POEMS: NEW & SELECTED

Marianne Boruch

Also by Marianne Boruch

POETRY

A Stick that Breaks and Breaks
Moss Burning
Descendant
View from the Gazebo

PROSE

Poetry's Old Air

poems
NEW & SELECTED

marianne boruch

Oberlin College Press
FIELD Poetry Series
Oberlin, Ohio

http://www.oberlin.edu/ocpress

Publication of this book was supported in part by a grant from the Ohio Arts Council.

Ohio Arts Council
A STATE AGENCY
THAT SUPPORTS PUBLIC
PROGRAMS IN THE ARTS

Library of Congress Cataloging-in-Publication Data

Boruch, Marianne.
    Poems: New & Selected / Marianne Boruch.
    (The FIELD Poetry Series v. 15)
    I. Title.   II. Series.

LC: 2003113329
ISBN: 0-932440-95-9   (pbk.)

Again, for David
again, for Will

CONTENTS

New Poems

II from *View from the Gazebo*, 1985

III from *Descendant*, 1989

IV   from *Moss Burning*, 1993

V   from *A Stick that Breaks and Breaks*, 1997

New Poems

THE HISTORY OF *THE*

first, we weren't anyone

or a cloud taught us. Then rain,
then the slow moving toward.
Which is to say, it was the sun
we saw, the sky
blue because certain vast machinery
in the eye tells us what is
color. Second, we found two whose
bodies might invite us here. Past
the dark room of that
though it was pleasant enough. Third,
the long slide. Then the longer
learning simple massive things: food
goes into the mouth. And on its way out?
Well, there are other things
of mystery: how one number equals those
two birds on a branch, why sleep comes
and forces you to lie down straight.
Remember, we weren't anyone.
And then, that changed
and changed again.

***

I had a book once

and opened it. Maybe it was important.
I watched my grandfather read like that, his lips
moved, silent, and I saw his eyes go
word by word, left to right. Forty years ago.

And to see that now? How could it matter?
Under the knife, the body is quiet.

And the surgeon gathers himself like water
to the sponge. The room is cool
as the past is cool in its
immaculate way. Dark hallways. Even in summer,
the rooms there.... Meanwhile, my grandfather
read by the window. And I gathered myself

though there was no self yet
to gather. How to say this? I watched
light fall on him and all his years:
beautiful, courtly.

***

the bone house

and we build it, one of childhood's
great triumphs. Rib, spine, femur, skull
to take the weight of days, release

of nights: knuckle, vertebrae, joints
for every movable minute—up, down,
in, out. Is the soul a tent

draped under it? Tiny fractures that
curve the spine, that change the walking
forward or backward, the cadence,

the way we imagine here to there.
Over so much time. And now this
stiffening, this clicking, each step,

each step down. Ghost of the old ones
passing into my tent where we
sit down wordless, no tea to pass.

***

the history of

the, says the linguist, began grandly
as *that.* As opposed to the plainest *a*
meaning a man, a woman, a day like any other
day between them. Oh ancient
the!—as in *that* second cousin I loved, say,
or *that* afternoon once, when you
looked down into the empty lot,
the old woman saying: sometimes, it's
just filled with cars! *The*
with a hat on, a wild feather
in such a hat, spotted, streaked,
even tipped in red. Until, until
the great graying into
the, oh lord of balance, oh
polite nod to center the blooming
whatever-it-is
on the tablecloth.

***

guesswork

is work: one eye open, the other—
always building back to that
earliest half-lit place
where days were an inch, the night
miles of inching through space,
one dim star
to star. I only mean

I liked those times
sitting in the woods alone,
nothing quite locked
in my binoculars, my confusion kept to
which bird and what flower
as if, for a moment, that
right on the verge of knowing were
a kind of knowing. So clouds
have no idea they're
clouds. The *almost* in us,
billowing.

                        ***

        snow melting on roof

isn't a halo. Isn't memory really
though in certain places, the shingles
next door—made to look old, that

cobble-looking old—show through
the way forgetfulness clears
for a second, and you're back

on the hospital stairs where
a nurse breaks down in tears,
looks up, startled—who were you

to be there? So much is unexplained.
It's all melting anyway—snow,
the thought of snow, its intrepid

invention: winter, that private
knock-knock no one answers, though
in bad poems, there's always

6

a voice for it, maybe a low moan.
In truth, it's merely cold
and cloudy—no glitter

off the roof's half snow.
No wind just now: sometimes
the mind stays here.

***

drawing, of course

I would draw my cat,
but she'd look back. I would
draw her but she's
way past sleep and sheds her
quiet like tickertape
down the long hallway, talking
cranky and offkey.

Of course, it's winter. I would draw
that, but a pencil isn't
fierce enough for branches stripped
to nothing. To one leaf, which
is as good as nothing. And nothing—
that gift needs invisible ink.

I'd draw the way words feel
in the mouth after too long without
words, or the way the body rises after
hours of dream, gravity
on every bone again, that anchoring
and ache.

Or I wouldn't. Or I couldn't.

Or I'd bury the treasure
in the most obvious place.

***

old photographs

take a moment and pretend
it's a life. The happy picnic. The happy
look-at-us amid flowers and soiled napkins.

My friend Joan took a picture once,
three nuns, all strangers in solid flowing white,
peering into the Grand Canyon, that

astonishing void. I see them
from the back, a hand just so, pointing.
A head tilted. There. And my eye, poor eye,

moves from one to the other to the other,
restless. And pleasure? The canyon's vast
and empty, and endlessly still. And so small,

my looking at their looking.

***

no one in the library this early

so it's all sleep, talkative
books silenced by their covers.
And xerox machines dreaming that

one rare uncopiable thing. And computers
still pinned to their home sites. Gladness is
human: none of that. Neither
is there sorrow, or sweetness, or—
no—no jubilation. And just to invite
tears into this place, one needs a full life
or at least one afternoon,
the traffic blinding someone
driving straight into the sun: *Officer,*
I just didn't see it. But is it solace?
Here? A quiet, clean corner. A book of poems
no one has touched for ten years. I open it
to the middle, a poem not
particularly good, maybe an afterthought
added the last few hours
before mailing off the manuscript.
Because one line, maybe
that one....

***

crossing the street at dawn

or not dawn, not yet. A few cars in the dark.
A young man with a backpack
in front of me. Stars? Too cloudy.
I left my car somewhere.
And walk. Too stiff to walk
this early. And the great university's halls—
looming sturdy as lament.
Across the quad, a door opens and closes.
The street lamps—one must
pass under them: the reverse
of shade. A kind of weird mist,
that light. So I let a pencil

bring it back, writing this by hand,
plain as it was: glowing, uneventful.

***

something flashes

in this hollow between buildings. Closer,
a notebook, smallest ambition
of the binding machine, big enough
to reduce the world to faded ink—one bird
and its color, say, someone carefully
writing the date: late winter, early spring.
Or it's just a phone number there,
no name. Mysterious
least of things, stained, open. One page
turning, turned back, this day
in a new century—one hour
or one life. It was mine, I'll say, or
it was yours. What do we call that?
Wind? Was that it?

***

really, I remember a window, nothing

special. A young tree flowered
once a year. The flowers pink, or they
were white, the stamens yellow
in the folds. Maybe the green finches

had turned their brilliant gold

by then, hanging funny on the feeder
to earn their thistle, seeds so tiny,
flying out of my hand though the wind—

hardly anything. A slow buzzing
of frogs those springs. At first we thought
insects, the pitch higher
on warmer evenings. I know exactly

when it stopped. By June or so, only birds
slowed the twilight, not
many. We sometimes walked then. It was
cooler, the sun out of the world, everyone

tired of the day and what it brought. What did
it bring? I remember only the same things
over and over, the way a song remembers,
coming back like that.

I

NEAR HALLOWEEN

Like a bad thought, someone else's
bad thought, it hangs
by the neck—stuffed jeans
and flannel shirt, the pillowcase head
grinning, before
it lops over.
               Student neighborhood. Which
jubilant drunk hoisted this thing
last night, from porch to star-eyed gable,
a toast: all sadness in the world—ha!
all misery—ha!—to you and you and damn you!
Below, the light of a car blurred
as it took the corner.
               The body turns
because there's wind. It turns
because it has no weight. The face goes
up, then down again, a soft thud
against the clapboards. It could be
anyone up there. And the leaves—their
thousands fall into the street, yellow wet,
rimmed with dark.
               Not that anything's eternal
or exactly like any other thing.

THE WAY THE DYING HEAR THINGS

The way the dying hear things, I don't know—
the nurse busy
with another patient, *now lift
your other leg*, voice too high,
vapid sweet.
     Or at some roadside crash,
blood pools secretly
under the coat, the *are you
all right?* urgent, polite. Is that
a serious question? Oh, to answer back!
To answer back....
      Everything must get
smaller to them, more stupid, more everything
it ever was. Once, in a lecture hall,
I watched the young professor lost, half-raging
unto the history of science stop
at radium, famous
bar of it in Curie's dresser drawer,
the dimmest corner lit until
in front of me, a student—middle-aged,
back-to-school—sagged, one
shoulder slipping.
     That's it. She
was gone. But *radium*, he said before
some of us behind her
started screaming. *Ra-di-um*, he kept
saying, echo
and ghost. She must
have heard that, so much
poison and shine.
     A day slips
through its needle, a toddler counts to seven.
Or flies *tap tap* in October, caught
between window and screen. The ear
isn't a flower though a poet might say so,
little hairs straight up
then leaning as any flower would
toward light.
     It's almost

night there. Down the twisted canal
go all sounds equal, the swearing
which ends soft
as prayer by the bed,
shit, dear god
damn it.

BAD CELLO

My bad cello! I love it
too much, my note to almost note,
my almost Bach, my almost Haydn, two who
heard things falling off a shelf—
they never thought that
was music. Try wind at night. Try that
against your good night's
sleep. Still, something's passing, same
as grief—there's no
word for it. Same as joy
but only in the flourish of up and down, the way
a note is held—or held off—
too long.
                    Certain afternoons are
private, forsythia against the window,
its hundreds of branches I should have
cut in summer, their
scratch-scratch-scratchity. So I practice
to them, so I practice
with them.
                    I keep thinking
how Brahms slept right through
my childhood, that print in a frame
above my grandmother's threadbare couch, and how
I loved his face completely. His eyes
were closed. He leaned against the piano.
And above him all those
other faces—Beethoven and Bach and Mozart—
misty currents they floated in said *dream*, said
go away, Brahms is having a vision right now,
said *Brahms needs his nap.*
                    It's just that—bad cello!—
the rondo? I like it, like to play it twice because
no words! Because *I do it*
so badly! Delicious part
going minor, right
down the hole, neither what-I-thought nor
what-I-dreamt. Dark in there. Strange.

ON THE STREET

The guy walking ahead, his boot
flares up, yellow
tulip tree leaf wet
to one sole, briefly, so brilliant,
then the boot's down again, then up
to the world, leaf intact,
and down to the dark, then back, bright
staccato all the way
up Pearl Street, turning—but I
still see it—down Vine.
                        And what to make of this,
this dismal November day,
the stark criss-cross of trees, the stray cat
starved again, heading
for the dumpster. But she's
wild. She won't let me near. And still
this perfect flash of something,
                        something
I say out loud, in the cold air.

LEAVES IN FALL

They come down, straight down or crooked,
fast or drunken. Wind might do it,
might call the cruel trick but they're
starving anyway, light's sugar
nothing so sweet now,
and then this mysterious business
of turning a drastic color. I rake.
I rake the damn sad things
all morning, past lunch.
What was I thinking?
                    That certain things
have to be done. That the earth
orbits slowly. That beauty gives up
its beauty. Huge piles of it—
maple's yellow, the elm's ghost gray,
hackberry with its sulfurous boils
curled tight. Maybe someone else
said this: the sky is a pearl, darkening.
Or this: it's bad milk, not a cloud
against anything.
                    So I rake
and drag it all on a tarp to the curb, the heavy
scrape scrape of it past birdbath
and trellis, past the cockeyed seasick mums,
past the torn shade of playroom, study, frontroom
where the old piano sits
completely out of tune. Dark inkling
it was, to the nether world
of the minor key.
                    The dead
lean forward....

DOUBLE DOUBLE

Where my son once slept, now
I write. These stick-on stars
flood the ceiling's slant, take in
light all day. It's a glowing night of it
at night. *Double double*, my brother
scribbled awkwardly up there, in pencil. His doing.
He put the constellations here. Below these twins—
whatever *double double* means—four stars
make a box. And then the pale green bits trail off.
Heaven's shapes are weird.
                                        Low, odd-angled room.
My son dreamt here—what?
Not even he remembers, his bedroom now
my old study, a trade
we made when he got too tall. In the house
next door, a baby cried non-stop
for years; older, that neighbor kid
still cries. And won't get in the car. Won't.
Never. And then he does.
And the car door slams.
                                        I wait all this. And wait,
to clicks of sparrow, the tuneless
finch—my window's up. *Write write!* because—
I don't know. Birds close down
for a fine few seconds.
                                        My brother's love was for
distant, burning places, my son's, simply
that the dark light up. But these stars
aren't stars. The ceiling
lies about it. This isn't endless space,
isn't the upper register of time where
timelessness is famous. Take a room.
Then quiet the world in there.
First, it's small.

SCIENCE, BOOK I

A seed on wet cotton. Next picture: a girl
stares, all greed and blankness, to pull
the pale shoot up. Down the page, a wooden board
has thrown a streak of grass
into dark—the boy is tentative, barely
lifting it. Worms—I swear—
love it under. And things with 30 legs,
a fiefdom.

So I walked into shade
for the millionth time: a porch, a sycamore raging
or standing still, one maple with its thousand
winged do-dads: all spoke their
tap tap tap to me. Six, or was I seven?
They said *heartbeat, come faster.* They said
rain on the attic roof. Tomatoes slept
into bursting overnight, poor vines bent,
on-the-verge-of, in the book or out of it.

Page 23. They're teaching us how cold
cold is. A boy takes off his coat,
then puts it on again. He's deciding something.
A man fiddles with the thermostat. Then it's
all about the cellar—his shovel
rising and falling, coal in bits, coal
that glows, the whole world
rearing up, great monster of the heat ducts
pouring its love into all the secret
spaces of the house.

No words. Everything slowed
by pictures. 1956 or '57. The quiet of
put-the-book-down-now. The quiet
of supper where the grail
held sweet milk. And the lamp was on.

PIANO TUNING

Of course, I left it, the tuning hammer
on the piano, and walked straight to the kitchen.
Left the old guy out there poised, bent
over it. Such a private thing
between them, the wooden panel open, hammer
to it, twin shafts on a maple handle. Something
about it—I couldn't watch—major,
not minor, then what the hell, back
to minor again, that underwater rush
going sharp and flat.

But I could feel it
in my chest. All morning, the pure
ache of it. And I did nothing in the kitchen,
that listening nothing, where you just
look out a window and watch for anything—birds,
grass bent at an angle. Because the whole time
it was the slow weight of the tuning hammer,
the metal strings that don't know
what music is, sweet
dumb narrowest expanse
of the deepest ore, singing out
its genius anyway.

I thought to do
other things—some cleaning up
or fixing a cold supper
for later. But I kept picturing
how it was out there, the tuning hammer
at the ancient upright. The old guy,
a genius himself in how he bent into it.
Again and again that private thing between them,
hammer to the strings, twin shafts, wooden handle.
I heard the turn and counterturn. It wasn't
love. But I heard
a shape—god, to know
what I was hearing—up, then down, forgiveness,
no forgiveness at all.

THE OLD MATHEMATICIAN

The mathematician, almost
too feeble to walk, walks down
Salisbury, over on Stadium, up Rose
or Robinson. No bird is an equation, not
the one in the tree, not the one in flight
with its wings crooked enough
to catch any updraft. And the tiny bones
in that darkness under the feathers—
no music's there. They aren't flutes,
hollow sticks that hold the body
barely, in wind or
no wind. But one bird equals how many
pebbles in the hand, equals equals
a small boy's anger to bring
something down. The kid just stands there,
fierce, ready. The mathematician
looks up. He looks sideways. I'm walking
through it, he thinks, some bad boy's longing
to be bigger, to be anything at all.
And then it multiplies. He can see it
in the underbelly leaf of the trash trees
no one's planted—there in the terrible boils,
the rusty edges. The sound of a shoe on pavement.
His or the boy's. Then, a door slams. Does it
matter? He gets livid at things.
Then he's vacant again. To add
and to subtract, back and forth
as he walks—it's a little
like breathing. Like someone digging a hole
and disappearing in it, spray
of dirt and stones, the shovel
glinting in rhythm. So I watched
one morning, not knowing which
sad business—the fury
or the indifference—larger in me.

IN WINTER

One headlight from my neighbor's car
cuts the yard in half, 6 a.m. No applause
from the two leaves
left on a branch, nothing from squirrels
high in their airsick nests.
From the stray dog,
it's zero and *nada*—he's shivering
somewhere in the alley. But really, it's
a thing you could almost lift, this light
in a tube, cheap
shaft of sun.
              And the elms? The elms
go weird with it, their great roots
lured up from the earth
to bathe radiant
before going down again.

PLEASURE

At the Art Institute, she's kissing him, he's
kissing her, centuries so far, or hours,
one era to the next. The terrible
earnest age with all its
crucifixions pressing finally—here!—
beyond the dazzling boulevard-out-the-window-
river years, French—who else?—always
looking at the distance
distantly, and eating. Believe me, these two
can kiss. Outside the ladies' room, they
kiss and touch each other's
hair and kiss again like underwater
a thing's caught quick
in running currents, and such
surprise. They aren't exactly. They're slow.
They haven't planned it. Still, this
bench is long and wide enough, big enough
for all of us, a back to it,
and sides. Not like some. Not like
my favorite in the room upstairs where
a whole field hovers, where Monet turned
on Paris and built his haystacks
winter, summer, in light
that autumn makes to lift us
back where failure keeps its pillow.
I half-lie there. And think
no thoughts. And then I
come down here. Of course, these two
are young, which is to say, I'm
not anyone, a piece of wood,
a wall. And they're
invisible.

SUMMER HOUSE

On the large porch, they're telling me
too bad it's cloudy, though the view
isn't ruined. They know too much.

One says, *he loves it here*, which
could mean any of the men on the grass,
an older one, a younger one, all

studying the slow drift
of the bocce balls: that red one
though now it's green's turn.

In the house, my son is
at the cello. He stops and starts: Bach,
not-Bach. It's almost

supper. A man comes up from the river
wiping his face with a towel.
One dog is deaf. She mistakes a voice,

wild with all the ways it isn't
what she knows. *Oh Tasha*, someone murmurs
and it's quiet, quiet again, just

the *clink* of the bocce balls
and a little Bach. *If only*, a woman says,
if only you were here earlier

in the week. *Yeah*, says another, *you
could have met so-and-so*. Oh summer,
which loves everything! We sit

for a moment in the dim thought
of missing whoever it was, savoring
this small misfortune.

BONES NOT OF THIS PUNY WORLD

Those saints, the ones
who sat high on poles, and looked down
half dizzy or with their eyes
shut, I think
about them, not constantly, just
occasionally, how seen from below,
they were wiry
bent shapes, which meant they were
praying, repeating some
fabulous, modest sentence—*forgive me,*
mother of all things that walk
or swim or fly, that think
or refuse to think—or they were
simply glazed over, going
lockjawed into that
holy blank. It was hot
in those places. People came in crowds
to look up, to exhort or to praise
or just to be part of the hardest
of landscapes, rocks
and scrawny trees, because those poles
were it, the center of life, like the quiet
blue-green iris can take
over the eye and float there and make it
famous. But what hopeless amoeba
is the mind after 35 years
on a pole, the sun past
blinding, *modesty forbids me*—past that,
because you've chucked
the clothes, you've
chucked the bits of childhood you might
have cherished, you've chucked
the walking around, taking to this one,
to that one, you've chucked
chucking anything so it's all
a vague blob you might, *might,*
nod to and then happily dream of, i.e.:
forget. Daniel the Stylite

(409–493), they had to break
his body when they finally figured out
he'd been dead three days. He came apart
too easily, like the old tinkertoys
my brother loved, small clicks at the joints
as they piled up bone and flesh,
reverently folding the cloth around it,
tying it with something—strips of leather,
or maybe they had rope by then.
Maybe they had a lot of things
by then: carts, and a few
hand-lettered books, emptiness
and anger, sadness for sure—*poor*
poor slob—or even irony
which lives in sadness
as a wing lives in certain insects
that can't fly but have
powerful legs whose needles flash.
And sharp like that, such irony—
sure, baked by God himself. No,
nobody talked like that—most of them
scared witless handling
bones-not-of-this-puny-world.
And the monks' lamentation? My *Oxford Book*
of Saints says it was "a clap
of thunder." But thunder follows
lightning and grows huge
on sudden air. And when the human weight
comes down? Wasn't there one guy
shaking his head
the way we walk around, shaking
our heads at every earnest foolishness,
people crazy the world
is ending on March 25th, say, who give away
their clothes and their cars, their
only good TV? I imagine
being Daniel sometimes. Past hunger
like that, past thirst, past

the sweetness of all that
giving up, how thin the body
can be, like paper one holds
to the light, and one's wish to be anything
even thinner than that.
What is desire anyway? A ribbon. A leaf.
A mechanical pencil. I *think*
about Daniel. How he looked down
from his altitude and saw people
looking up, amazed or indifferent,
and after a while going off to wherever
people go. Then there was
nothing down there in the dark but the road,
and mostly no road, just the tired expanse
of desert, no line between earth
and not-earth. Some nights, such stars
came out that he looked up, but not
to love them. I think about that—
not to love them—and the sky goes
brilliant in bits that drift
nowhere, and are steady,
and give no sign.

AT HORTICULTURE PARK

They make a great noise in the leaves,
trying to be quiet, these
ROTC boys, to be stealth
as the bomber eaten
by fog. Their faces
smudged black, their slow
passage under maples, under
the huge oaks. It's fall,
its wild ravishments. Everything's
past camouflage into almost
freeze and rest
and the last thought. They do not
look at my son and me, where
we might walk, or where
we've been in these woods.
And their emptiness, which is
a kind of focus, they practice it
like prayer, like the sad violinist, fierce
and without any hope
of song, climbing his C minor scale
for the twentieth time. Afternoon nearly
lost to twilight. They look—where else?—
perfectly ahead. A line
is a line. And their rifles, even
the smallest—I watch him—holds his
not gently, hard against him.
Oh, to be
a threat, to swallow
anything. *Dear boy, go home.*
Go home, where you left your longing.

THE DRIVEWAY

next door. A mother to her
children *put that down*, and *I
said*, and *Did you hear what
I said?* And the small voices like
flowers blown back by wind
rise up, not really music,
not words, a high pitch of shrug,
and looking away, and looking
down where the ground is
suddenly interesting. The day
is summer, passing without
any weight at all, like water
loves the hose, and stains
its dark channel.

SONG IN SPRING

The young who shield their eyes from the sun
in their teens or just out of it, aren't
all that young. They take big steps. They think
what now and *should I* and *fuck you*.
The *fuck you* is the easy part, yolk of an egg
that loves the sizzling grease, mouse
the trap dreams of, the way cars
veer off at dark, all headlight until
the curve in the road swallows them. Such
relish. But the *what now*, and the *should I*,
that's the loneliness straight. And how many
days and nights, years of that before the body
tells none of its secrets gracefully
but gets used to things broken, an ache
in the rib each morning, the singing
knee, the jaw that clicks and jumps
its joint, to come back barely. Oh, that
Fuck you in the bright afternoon. Child
with the foul mouth, darkly radiant on the steps.
New leaves maneuver each bud, the blinding
bicycles speed by.

I IMAGINE THE MORTICIAN

I imagine a mortician looks at the hands
first, the lines up toward the fingers,
then down toward the fleshy parts, how
one crevice crosses at an angle
and stops. I imagine this on a summer day.
Or I imagine myself walking early morning,
really early, when it's still half dark,
imagining with each step that poor
mortician in some cool room across town
faced with a slug of a thing—no one
he knows—merely weight now. Or perhaps
I *was* walking, but the thought
stopped me. I didn't dare
look at my hand, its own
scattered lines, webs that go nowhere.
But the mortician? Probably
a bored one too, one who half-hates
his job, whose father and grandfather
made him, he had no choice, not really,
though the hands—they are
interesting, aren't they? It might be
a hobby of his that perks up the whole
awful business, gauging the lifeline
against the real life, watching the years
stop short, then bringing the body
back to the world in his dream
of that body, flashing it back to the yard,
bright sun, garden shears, blackberries.
I walked this morning—that's
the truth of it. How was I to know? The air
only gradually gave up its dark. My mind—
only birdsong entered, sound
like pebbles tied together with string
and trailing off. So I let
the mortician in
with his bent curiosity, the reverse
of the new mother who counts
all the toes and fingers
and is so relieved.

MY UNCLE WHO HATED ZOOS IS

at the zoo—okay: orangutans, albatross, a lion
perfectly bored in her stretch. To that
he closes his book.
                            How long have I
been dead?
                    Years, I say, *fif-teen-years*—dramatic, distinct,
three stresses adrift in the silence.
                                        And my wife?
                    Virginia? I say.
And my house?
                    A beautiful house, Uncle
though I never saw the last one. Was it
beautiful? Is a squid beautiful?
Is the unbearable reptile whose name—
some tangle in Latin—I can't even pronounce?
I keep nodding. Things get darker
in autumn. You say things anyway, exactly like
leaves do their fall thing
assbackwards in wind, billowing up
after coming straight down. You'd think
they'd stay put. And those trees in the distance,
I'm squinting to read them, their one bright
sadness at a time.
                    My book! he's
almost shouting. Oh, the wide creature racket
of this place, the honk honking, the caw
cawing. He looks down, quiet.
And honest to god, my dead uncle's
reading—say it's *Guilliver's Travels.* Or say
my dead uncle's on page 72
of *Ulysses.* I'll tell you this: my dead uncle
loves Ambrose Bierce.
                            Uncle? But he's lost to me now.
Do the dead forget? Is it like me
in a dream once, telling my one sweet cat—
Go on, go home now. I already have
a cat. *Forget, to forget*, this *forgetting* thing
all over the place.

I look it up. "To cease
from doing." But one *does* that, right? One
"ceases from doing." You *do*
to *do not*. Inedible phrase!
Dreamsick oxymoron!
                              i.e.: Forget
the house. He's the one
who's beautiful, sitting there in his bathrobe
as if this were a porch, a veranda, a certain
rest-his-soul lanai
near a landslide or something.

SMALL YARDS

To get the whole world in there: not just
the mold-sweet birdbath, dry since June. Not simply
the plastic deer broken at the knee,
hoisted to its heroic stance
by a large, rather unpleasant-looking, pockmarked
rock. The world is
richer, way beyond the young man—black or white—
red tails and cap, racist-tacky
or merely tacky, forever offering his lantern
to these autumn days. And what about those
multiple, multi-colored pinwheels
lined up against the weather? Or the shadow guy?
A cutout, no expression, no soul
or whatever passes for it
as he putts the ball across the stillborn, never-
to-be-green concrete of some driveway. A sandtrap?
An imagined sandtrap? He's hopeful still,
if you need a narration. And then, next door
(a sale one time? a 2 for 1?) another shadow guy
climbs a ladder nowhere, his flattest
of brushes raised to paint nothing really, the eternal
bliss of the about-to-be, etcetera, etcetera, world
upon world. Because the whole world
is never whole. Didn't I
know that? But those pink flamingoes. Or the twisted
bonsai, tortured into beauty and grace. Grace!
To get that you might wish a lifetime
at the little well with its little wooden bucket
wound up tight, its depth not
a lake's but a pocket's. A pocket? Magical, who-knows-
what-one-might-find-there, a pocket's
good, yes? It will do, yes? Answer: no.
Answer: I'm just
in my car sometimes. And I see things.

WIRES

Blue wires, gray wires, wild massive
bundles wrenched from outer space somewhere,
and scattered in the hall. Men do this. Men
who talk on walkie-talkies to someone

who gravels, blinks out, gravels back.
Walking by, all of us suddenly so
careful. Outside, it's merely a few
leaves. A sky. Too much concrete. But here,

the men love talking to little machines,
the matter-of-fact of it, an old giddiness
shrunk down, hand to ear, the curious way
a face looks, tilted, with nothing

yet to say. Blue wires, and gray. The thought
and the afterthought. Both enter the ceiling
but *nothing connected yet*, the larger man says,
bewildered, somehow stricken. In truth,

it's the drinking fountain I walk to,
or the xerox which hums and makes too much
of everything. This tangle of wire—savor it,
like any small chaos, hair left

in a brush and you pulled out the whole
mess of it. Or the tiny what-was-that
one of us found, bending down, pointing.
A nest!—we looked up. No tree in sight.

LITTLE FUGUE

Everyone should have a little fugue, she says,
the young conductor
taking her younger charges through
the saddest of pieces, almost a dirge
written for unholy times, and no,
not for money.
              Ready? she tells them, measuring out
each line for cello, viola, violin.
It will sound to you
not quite right. She means the aching half-step
of the minor key, no release
from it, that always-on-the-verge-of, that
repeat, repeat.
              Everyone should have a little fugue—
I write that down like I cannot write
the larger griefs. For my part, I
believe her. Little fugue I wouldn't
have to count.

ELEGY

Before the basil blackened. Before plates
slept in their cupboard. Before the streets
were snow. Before the song started in the throat
or crept sideways into the hands that hold the cello
or the moon spilled to nonsense all
over the floor. Before color composed itself
to twenty names for blue, or was it green or was it
red? Before seeds entered the ground
to transform themselves. Before cake was eaten, before
the icing bubbled up and crystallized. Before
all that sugar. Before shells
when things were moving in them and the sea
made a noise. Before our son grew so eye
to eye. Before worms made their fiefdom
in the compost. Before sleep refused the night
and the clock kept ticking. Before the hospital
took the soul from the body, dark
from dark, and the long drive home. Before the dog
stopped mid-bark to bark and the cat rose
from her stretch, unblinking. Before every moth
in the flour stilled its wings. Before the stain,
before its memory in the wood
grew wider. Before the garden gave everything
to weeds. Remember that, O charm
to forget, to go back, to vanish? Before
the dead appeared at the edge of my vision. Before
the grace to be broken was broken.

ALL THOSE PEOPLE

earnestly talking to themselves
in elevators, on bikes, or walking
any street, with dog or without. I see
their heads turn slightly. And the veil
between us thins to a world
welling up. No one's ever jubilant, talking
to himself. Take the guy in the parking lot,
arms out, pleading to a ghost.
And everything human floods over
and under. The word
pity back to *pittance*, something passed
in embarrassment, flashing briefly
before it drops to the dark
of a pocket.
                    And those perfectly
reliable types, going to work in outfits,
at red lights, in cars, holding forth to no one,
gesturing *this*, then *that*. Or lips
barely moving on those who live lost
in themselves. Sweet. Furtive.
And my own car? I talk into the steering column
all the time. The heating vent, it knows my heart.
And windshield wipers? *Old story, old story,*
pathetic downbeat.
                    The most ancient woman
on earth limps by. She's talking too! How peculiar
we all are. Imagine the imagination, some
curious box way back in the brain, springing open at
—childhood? trees and rivers?
right and wrong? heartache? starlight? brakes
giving out, oh speeding car.... In fact,
we deserve nothing. But will this
remember-wheel, this thought-so-secret, whatever
odd-sad-thing-in-there
say something amazing? Will it
talk back? Listen. Way back. Quiet. Please.

ONCE AT BERGHOFF'S

So forty years later, I cross autumn
as usual, its elegant distortion of fact—
that window, Chicago's old downtown, a girl
and her mother at lunch in that understated
stately place. Which is to say, cloth napkins.
Which is to say, the sky darkened, made
lamplight by buildings. Exactly
as my mother dreamed.

Not without a scene, of course. A linen dress
I didn't want, its overwrought embroidery,
flowers weeping their tiny
busy opera. Finally, I liked the waiter
—you like the waiter, don't you? my mother said—
the way he held himself so secret
in a hoarse ironic whisper.
I hadn't thought intelligence that austere.

Rain, it seemed, for weeks,
and then the day before, it cleared.
That was autumn too, and city apartments
lived in years, buildings mortgaged
and double mortgaged, windows that launched us
into streets staggered with leaves, piled high
by boys who worked by the hour, or cousins,
brothers, because they were told.
Leaves by the curb crested on sidewalks,
on fenders. And fathers coming out of kitchens
with matches, then the smoldering fragrant
eclipsing smoke. Everything lit
and sending up signals.

Coming home, my mother stepped off the bus
so gracefully that afternoon. Our real street
flared up, all red leaf and haze, kids
somewhere shouting. Forty years now,
forty years—I watch her turn
and speak politely as a stranger
to the driver.

SIN

In that airless box, it fell from us like rain
though backwards, up, past all clouds
to light. Or so Nancy Allen swore
earnestly, tenth in our Confession line,
face close to my face, the perfect lamb
in any story, her big eyes
black, her fuzzy hair so blond it wasn't
blond but pure daylight
off a holy card. *Girls, no talking*—that
quiet, deadly hiss five
pews away. And Nancy, most rapt of looks,
blinked out.
        I looked inward
where nothing stirred. The box loomed closer.
I pushed to count each awkward lie,
each mean forgetfulness, each *talk back*
in my little life on Argyle Street
not little, not now, not
when every sin burned brightly in hell if I
died this minute without Confession,
my heart, simplest of creatures,
giving up its creaturehood. *It could happen,*
Nancy might have breathed, selflessly
adding sin to sin by talking.
        Dark church because
of thunderstorms all morning. And weeks
into Lent, a double whammy. Boys
went first because they, of course, were
worse. *Boys, your need*
is greater, is how the nuns discreetly
put it. And Darrell O'Connor
or James Padinski—I watched them
up the line fidget in their pockets
which held such treasure. Not coins
but metal slugs that fit the hand and pressed
a raw, red circle there, or marbles
shining their mute
cat's eye. Girls had no pockets

in those uniforms—singular
injustice! We came
as is, and kept no secrets, sure.
Another awful sin
is envy.
            It wouldn't be
so long. I silently rehearsed
my *Bless me, Father, for I have sinned*
and reran my count as Nancy
floated next to me, her eyes closed
to keep it all miraculous
and private. And that heaven thing?
In fact, I stood there,
nothing more. Even so, I love that
in the world. A whole life's
passed since then.

II

from *View from the Gazebo,* 1983

VIEW FROM THE GAZEBO, 1914

Late June & the bees came
violent, rising off the far hedge
in busy black hooks.
We too were busy,
lemonade busy, day to day
and porchlight busy,
so busy we thought them
hummingbirds
that nervous race
which overruns the afternoon
with wonder, graceful creatures
soundlessly
emptying the rose.
Such stillness.
My father closed his book
with a low whistle.
These bees
finding our clover thin,
our thickets barely ripe
angered. In the silent brain
of the gazebo, my parents froze
elegant & empty-handed,
Victorians at the edge of sleep.
This heady mob rushing toward us,
an ancient mesh, dark and light
crushed against the wind, I thought
the world is ending.

THE BLUE-BLACK LIGHT

A child with a gun
is parting the bushes next to the house,
his foot dropping steadily
over stones, over darkened grass.
Breathing is difficult as the moment
nears
       I put down my book
in this blue-black light, as if water
could or needed to be
read. What was I thinking: *remote,*
possible. I know that
stirring, how quick it happens.
Now the child
slipping out of the leaves,
not a shadow at all
but a thought
         slipping out of its mind,
sucking up the room
as I sit swearing I
haven't heard a human voice for years.
The trees wild, small winds
ruthless in their courage,
         the child
trembles on the walkway.
         What shiny
thing in the heart surrenders
or is opaque.

DIAMOND BREAKFAST

Overnight, the windows have multiplied & eaten
the house. Boom! everything
is thinner, everything
manic with light. "Whirling dervish!" whispers
mother, screwing up her eyes
into little eyes. The children
lean like cactus in the doorway. Maybe
they are missing school. O rodeo, O Oklahoma shimmer.

Father clears his throat. "Things
are different now," he says, addressing the squints
from the breakfast nook. "That stove, for instance,
these eggs—all just a glimmer
of their former selves. Remember this.
This is like history." One boy agrees. He is
shielding his eyes as if an iceberg
has surfaced, he is planting
a blue flag.

Now they are eating, drinking: glossy oatmeal,
shiny milk. Everything is a ghastly color. White & white
& white again. Outside, birds dive
into invisible walls,
their small heads dashed against pure thought.

THE VIOLINIST BEGINNING TO FLY

—after Chagall

They plan to get him down,
a loop of thread
pulled from his trousers and the only way
says the doctor
of willfulness and logic, a coppery icon
rooted and lit
above the leather bag growing
smaller as we walk away.

From this distance, the violinist is drifting
straight into the sun: just a man
fiddling his brains out, say—joy bundle of nerves,
say—man disbelieving the dark secret, say—rooflight
in a bottle and he's drinking it.
Think about his heartbeat then, slow as anyone's
who, searching and searching, finds
the perfect place to live. These bits of Handel
bracing the air, or letting it go, not
going to the dogs but just stepping outside: here

a dazed summer night, the screen door
banging behind, lily of the valley in the walkway,
inevitable smell of rain. Ah—so many things, finally

not to care about.

LOVE POEM AGAINST THE SPRING

Spring means nothing but camouflage
so we dare to say these corny things. Irrelevant birds
smokescreen up the afternoon & purple flowers
rear up their idiot faces along the sidewalk's edge.
Ok, they're cute. My hunger's not, nor my ache
at you green-leafed and alert somewhere, not here.
Perhaps the pretty air
exaggerates some things. I see, a friend annunciates,
you *access* him, as if you were a computer.
Last night I saw three couples, incredible throwbacks,
strolling into dusk, two so giddy, they'd love everything.
I'm quiet as a brick. But for spring,
this far I'd go—glad, I guess, to shed this coat. It's you
I crave, you who get more stunning
as we age.

A LINE IS JUST A SERIES OF DOTS

I was swelling up with Euclid
my sophomore year. Our thick tweed jackets

hung like captured ghosts. It seemed
a winter book: face value, spare,

fueled by white bones. Next to me, Curry
popped jellybeans in her Twiggy cut, daydreaming

roses or rowdy John York. But I was
heartsure, floating in the third seat, these

were magic tools: protractor & compass. Did they
shine in the dark? I never looked. I knew.

Sister Francis gummed her words. "It doesn't happen
happenstance." And we, alert as blue grass,

stared into the eerie page where triangles & squares
held their breath in open air. This is

our secret life, I thought, as line moved
onto line, as gardens focused

in the awful mist. I was swelling up
with Euclid, pure thread all that endless spring,

trailing proofs to their treasure, an inevitable
cloud, an inevitable clearing.

THE CHEERFUL LIGHT OF JULY

The solemn luxury of a fall day
is memory already, birds sepia
in their certain journey out of sight. We look up
cold morning, afternoon, the gray sweater weight
thinning the trespass of wind and stupidity.
I'm imagining this
in summer as leaves gaze blankly into sun,
as kids downtown
skateboard the minutes
until supper and it's still light outside
as we eat. I hate summer, which is beauty
so transparent, a wealth so true and trusting
I cannot believe but backdrop,
bright easel to narrow in the wharf, the fleeting boats.
I think: snow, snow and the mind
invents storms that come, leaves
turning violent, red and yellow
out of sheer boredom
with the slow pitch of a summer month.
I put on my shoes and go outside.
Cheerful light of July where no death creeps
which makes me nervous—these boats
taking their time on the perfect lake, ferry
their pleasure out, then home again
and so disguise, disguise, disguise.

WE DROVE

to the end of the world in a real
nice car, red upholstery
and the gasoline scent of childhood filling
the whole backseat with darkness
and lemonade and the drive-in already
starting, screen flicker
of power and bosom, Dad lifting the bright box,
hero-voice
spurting into the old Chevy.
We had these pale pajamas, curling
sideways, we followed the beam
through its gaudy lifetime,
blue-greens focused
then blurred,
a lady's red lips flung
open against the final second. We knew
nothing of this, or the moon's
double color, jouncing every which way

home, silent, half-
happy the thing over and sleep
a real one
taking off his hat, past railroad
dumps, houses here and there
glowing in the fields,
Dad's filibuster of neighbors
and melancholy friends, the wide
road, everything
winding down
to a pin, the original
night.

LETTER

When the final cricket stops
—a few moments ago,
this part word, that part
nothing refinable—
what is written
lengthens: the light
of the moon's rare
thought. Yesterday I thought
you'd be whistling toward me
delighted as usual
with a simple supper—rice,
bits of beef, something
thin and leafy.
I sensed you coming
a moment ago. I almost
heard your whistle,
some fine Puccini knife
cutting the whole
dark, field
cramping up behind you,
a heavy bulk
chewing up your passage
which was light
as usual, musical.
The crevice deepens
around the house. Yesterday,
half-earth, half-air, workmen
stood and blankly shoveled
in the sun. I bolted out
of sleep with this, as if
the drift had started,
as if the neighbor's house,
the field you love
had dwindled, and
in the distance, darkened.
Step wide
when you return
too late to see
this thing which
strangers dug
which scares me.

HER BROWN CHECKED DRESS

I open the door to this room
flooded with childhood, *just going about our business,*
my grandmother before the dresser mirror,
curling iron in hand.
I am the girl, twirling on the tall footboard,
just a kid, a punk
watching as a child watches: how long till supper,
till sleep, till school. She is small.
She steps into a brown checked dress, smoothing it down,
bony thing, hopeless
to look right, she says, giving it up, taking powder
to her face. My uncle's young
and in a frame,
smiling as he never smiles. I am telling about
Vickie and what she said to Glenna
about that boy. We discuss it carefully, the way
chess is played
on a deeply shadowed porch. Midsummer, 1959,
and I become a ghost to find her.
Here is my body.
Here are my useless shoes.

STRANGER IN YOUR ROOM

Late that day, old woman,
nothing pulsed. The bike got stiff.
Long miles, I ached it
home, up the freezing driveway,
paused, past your window where
you read as usual,
the hazel glow of lamp
all winter, words
you stubbornly

clung to. But the curly-headed stranger
poised in twilight
on the pale divan, only
I could see him
across from you, his head
in his hands, thinking
past something, past: *should I?
is she that...?*

I stepped back—moment neither
here nor in some afterlife, half
second where Charon
poled his boat and poled his boat
and poled his boat....
How carelessly you turned the page!
As if roof
could hold the dark dead weight,
wind up, snow
shifting so
against the house.

DISTANT KNOWLEDGE THAT SPITS AND FLASHES

Whatever distance a man considers,
he picks up the telescope
to change it. I would bring you closer
if I could, as flipping on the radio
brings the 18th century into the room: Bach
wallpaper and oranges, old bedspread
and scissors of Bach, suddenly
corduroy of Bach turning into a shirt
as I fiddle with the bobbin
against the cold teeth of this machine.
I think of the machine
that took you, dazzling car
midwinter, and I think you back centuries
before words were invented
to explain your death, or the car, or the broken asphalt.
Angel of logic, distant knowledge
which spits and flashes. Change it if I could,
picking up this telescope
to zoom you back, here
for a simple talk
but there are stars where you are.
Their passion blinds you.

FALLING ASLEEP TO VOICES

A room drifts into evening like a boat
is slow, carrying up a long sadness
from childhood,
those two silver oars.
I can barely make them out,
straining to remember
as furniture disappears,
as voices of neighbors
up from the yard below
go laughter, go so many stones upon a bell,
fish within fish
until all of it is water.
I'm sure now, sure
I've been floating like this
every summer for 33 years.
I lie down in it. I close my eyes,
rising on the disembodied sound—leaves too,
hesitant in the wind,
a hammer falling, a child bouncing a ball.
Lovely world
which has no body, just voice, just
darkness, what we crave in it,
distance—a curse
as blurred as a kiss,
as splendid, as irrelevant.
I pull the covers up,
hoping this is death.

THIS MOMENT OF RAVEN

I stand in the middle of the road
but I don't know it's a road.
Only in hindsight is this possible.

Saying then, I stood in the middle of the road,
leaf-light but thickening
with summer as a man up ahead

walks beside his horse   *it's all right, steady*
taking the hand
of the child beside him. In hindsight then,

I imagine this 100 years ago, this
in hindsight, that it's sensible
for a man to calm a horse

that carries him, the child who
will bury him but tenderness
clouds the moment

out of hindsight into this raven
who takes me into his heart
whispering: watch this man this horse this child,

you know them.

MEMORY BISCUIT

Everyone's real world is a memory biscuit
lodged somewhere past all thought
or near the ribs—a question of how one
sits when a strange kid is howling
and you're thinking: *my* kid will be interested
in the classics.

Meanwhile, the biscuit dreams,
pulp of childhood and lumpy adolescence
nudging its way to the table
after years
of hanging around: just the kitchen, just
the corny backyard.
Voila! a four-course dinner
under American trees. What a bang
to start with—lime jello on lettuce. Sometimes
everything on earth
seems edible. Sometimes everyone in you
is eating.

BIRD CENSUS

The town was obsessed with birds,
how many and who and wherever
they went during winter. An ad in the *Courier*
begging for bird-wise, sensible shoes, we will pay,
please appear with a solid lunch, all
sighters who dapple the woods with their sneaky love,
a sudden breath
at the flash of a heron bathing
where the forest drops from ordinary wonder, but
I paraphrase, grow waxy. They were, in fact,

a ruthless bunch: Mr. Sausage
& rugged Long John and the larger mad librarians
of every age. But my Peterson! My opera glasses!
I was awestruck, stuck at the end of the line, through pines,
then maples, they discussed ferns, or dark remains
of ferns: *Matteuccia Struthiopteris, Onoclea Sensibilis*, I thought
Virgil's calling his sheep home as we Romans
forge. Britain! Horrible Snow!
endless and oh, what a night,
our rations low, Captain, O Captain, our
fearful trip is done, done! Duck!

shot Aragon Pound, and the Quaker Lady, second-in-command,
lowered her hand. We held our silence
like a box of mints. It didn't look
like a duck. I crouched in the unpronounceable
bones of foliage. Killer red, my brother would call it,
holding his hand to his eyes, peeking was piercing
color in that shaded rush of snow. A small bird
idled. What *was* he doing? Thinking, probably, having
a nice dream: worm sandwiches, sugared water
for all. I wasn't that

crazy about him. He looked obnoxious really, as if
the redder reds had huffed: all right for you,
Pill. Still, he didn't startle.
Stage Presence. I admired that, a form of belief

not at all embarrassing in a bird. But it was me
who wondered, caught between air and water,
not knowing how to swim or fly. I eyed
the other watchers eyeing him, their fabulous strain,
inaudible pencils: female, young, indicates
hundreds of others. "Hundreds" in this

drowsy wasteland? A wacky over-
abundance of human hope. I hoped they'd gone
south, Gidget feasting on eggrolls & Moondoggie
whisking off the blanket for the 89th time. Ah, such crumbs!
Beer, baloney and rye. In the distance, more
distance, the sea rattling its light and secret and a whole slew
of killer reds hoarding the rocks
in a single-minded sate. My god, who were these people.
I felt instant gloom. A bird exception. Bird blues. I didn't have

a pencil. Shhh! one said. The bird began to move,
fanned out, a blur
of red pitched into the branches. She began
to sing. But they never sing, Aragon
hissed, the Quaker thumbed
her book, Long John trembled: maybe it's
a different sort of bird.
                    Maybe it's not a bird at all, I said,
too gaily. They reported only
my shoes: *not sensible.*

ON TRANSLATION

The hungry man in the blue hat
has borrowed his ghost   no
the ghost in the borrowed hat just
sat down to dinner. The dinner's really something,
is, all extraordinary, it is, more than that, well,
a secret, shhh!—a lobster who did not die of fright.
"So this one went willingly!" says the ghost
with the borrowed tongue. "Oh yes oh yes oh yes,"
chants a chorus of waiters pressing a bright fork
into his hand. "Ah, such a big one," thinks the man,
"and such a little fork!" He is eating now,
reading between bites, a small round book.
Perhaps the ghost of a book. It is hard to describe
but suddenly, as I watch, I see
the ghost of a lobster beneath the blue hat
rising, rising on a wave
which curls into itself. Something's haunted
twice, in such a mouth.

I PUT ON MY JONATHAN EDWARDS
THIS APPLE SEASON

There it is, simplifying the table, everyone
sitting down to apple pie, a pie
reaching back beyond the crust of human anything,
a pie of knowledge we invented words for: *knife fork pie tin*.
But I put on my Jonathan Edwards & sit
alone, October 23, 1749.
What does it take really, to see
the wolf in that bewildered docile dog
sleeping near the fire? I pick up the napkin again, think
fear fear in that dog's eye
as the wolf creeps unsteadily
from the doggy heart.... The whole
country, sitting down this minute:
a sliver, a la mode, with cheddar. O ancestor,
lowered right now from the tree, a thought
wrenched from the gloom & glowing darker.

CHICAGO POULTRY

We are fighting because the
man walking around the Loop
with the chicken on his head, that guy,
I swear, he's got a chicken and, snot, you say
over and over, No   No   as to a child,
it's a duck it's a duck it's a duck. And I
hoard the table with a terrific shout.
Fuck you. It's a chicken. I know a chicken
when I see a god-damn fucking chicken. I
grew up eating chicken, being chicken,
playing chicken, two legs and two heads
in that god-awful teenage water at Foster
Avenue beach. That's what I hate about you,
you tell me right in the face, right in the eye,
right under our immediately precious roof.
WHAT   I shout through the silent bottom bible
of the courtroom stack. Your roots, he
said, are so mediocre.

LETTER FROM TAICHUNG

You ask how it is.
I can say not good, or
all good, only I am

too lonely, a shut window
the rain beats
blankly against.

Beauty is—
dangerous: whisper of snakes
all summer, their fine poison

flashing through the body
but today, November first,
I picture all venom

quietly into sleep. The snake
coiling
under winter's rock

is comfort. You can see
my slow head.
The weather comes cooler,

rain in the air,
memory
keeping the ruin

alive. Who felled the wall?
I have been reading
an old book

whose cover rots
as I find my way, its spine
shattering

into my lap, the words
Marcus Aurelius, over
then over again:

we are breath
bones vanish
forget the imagination.

I ride the bus
into Taichung,
the unbearable swell,

crowds, motorcycle
& bicycle swarm, all color
a blur of color.

Forget the imagination.
This is merely
a bus, cutting

through the raving
world. Chaos
is enough—the old ghost

tires beside me—float
lightly to death
upon it.

THE FORTUNE TELLER

The rest of my life is disguised
in my hand, any intelligence
but mostly confusion
stalking over it, Sumerian tracks
found in some tedious dig
near the holy land.
                    There is a woman now
poised over it. I remember
a dark cloud coming up fast
& dry fields
              corn, soybeans waiting
in a dim happiness. I say
happiness—ridiculous, of course.
Their disguise is what we read, that
faint shiver, leaf-pulse   root   then
rain beginning.

THE HAMMER FALLS, IS FALLING

All morning, the man roofs the house
he has dreamt the night before,
walking with the wood in his hands
which is growing
as he holds it. The hammer falls, is
falling, one knee bent, he
slams the nail
into its silence & out again into the great world,
bird, rushing
out of sight, only
a black wing, the look of a wing,
a glimpse of its darkness, nothing.
Stupid, he
bends his knee, stupid. Still the hammer
falls, is falling & the child
he dreamt, putting her to bed, closing the door
under the rude stars, is beginning
to wail, to call up
a word, the man hearing on the roof
the sound of the nail turned bird turned pupil
of darkness, watching the air as though
it were breathing.

A THIN DARK ROOM

this is your heart, I think.
By its brooding, by its simple pain,
I know it as a gregarious child
knows loneliness, the life below streets,
that sleepwalk
among gasworks and waterlines.
I was that child as you were that child,
bodies spent and curled stubbornly
around that vast bleak distance underground,
the unhappiness in our heads
brought up hard against it
as a woman matches fabric, square
by various square, against
a recalcitrant brotherhood, the solitude of thread.
Then you turn in sleep.
Shades begin to leak their light.
I watch the smooth beauty of your back
take form, bearings of bone loosen
then nudge tight.
This too is your heart: fall of sun
cold, distinct,
the old groundwork
buried gradually and clean.

SYMPATHY

I drag this big bed to the window
which takes years probably
as garden spills, as birds darken,

the tree outside
slips into her farthest ring, heave
of new bark, water, wood air.

I think she listens so
near the window, pressing
her strange light. I sing

o ragged quilt over the whole world,
meaning to say: such is my simple grief,
this great dim street

glistening with boys.
How their mothers thin them down,
calling them home,

quiet baseballs, a few
blue stones. What secrets
in a boy, pitching the last gladness

high into evening: curve,
cut, I hear it fallen
at the window, crying to be let in.

III

from Descendant, 1989

MY SON AND I GO SEE HORSES

Always shade in the cool dry barns
and flies in little hanging patches like glistening fruitcake.
One sad huge horse
follows us with her eye. She shakes
her great head, picks up one leg and puts it down
as if she suddenly dismissed the journey.

My son is in heaven, and these
the gods he wants to father
so they will save him. He demands I
lift him up. He strokes the old filly's long face
and sings something that goes like butter
rounding the hard skillet, like some doctor
who loves his patients more
than science. He believes the horse

will love him, not eventually,
right now. He peers into the enormous eye
and says solemnly, I know you. And the horse
will not startle nor look away,
this horse the color of thick velvet drapes,
years and years of them behind the opera,
backdrop to ruin and treachery, all
innocence and its slow
doomed unwinding of rapture.

A DECK OF CARDS THROWN TO WIND

The treehouse was my heart
and the flung cards children tore and left
my levitation. It was neither wind
nor joy. It was more
my sorrow which held them high
and made them swim midair.
I watched them
from the porch, blank
with that little endless afternoon
which took years
to get through, childhood, and the backyard
rich in trees. But beyond, the stunted crabapple,
violent, taking aim.

When I passed my neighbor's barn today,
there was one bale
suspended, creaking only a little
as it swayed and burned
a shadow of itself on the slow cold floor.
It pinned my eye, and I stood

like a kid, released
into the cruelty of things.

THE FOX

Someone was kind and poisoned the fox,
a bright hour for setting out the flag
to warn, saying sweetly, here fox
here. O cloud,
inviting darkness
to the moon. I stopped the car
and wandered in that wood
an hour, to another life,
a fox bloated
and no longer a fox
but a window in that room
years ago, where ashtrays
never emptied, where you smiled and shrugged,
where neither of us knew enough
to tell the truth. Sweet poison
in those years was sweet enough
to linger on and on.
We invited darkness
there. You said, clouds
cover the moon too much.
A man set a red flag against the tree
not a mile from that window.
We didn't know yet
what such flags mean. We said
how pretty against those leaves.

BUICK

On the rusting fender of the old
Buick, I lay down my head
and watch the field blur with flowers.
Clouds in their noble boredom
drag the sky bluer as they

pass. But this is winter, and I'm inventing
what leads me out of my life,
a set of intricate pulleys, gift
of the boy genius in the basement—my brother
maybe—who begged off school to get on with things.

Nothing shakes this field: eventually
shadows sift into grass, earth
cools by evening, and not like music.
This Buick was my father's. I'm sure of that.
He drove it here drunk. He parked it here

gracelessly, and sat with years
bunched up behind him, which is to say
he thought of nothing, squinting down
the glare. So my family figures things. We stop
until the fury dwindles down to ash, what

would be bone. Perhaps an archaeologist could
find us. One xeroxes an unreadable something
through the winter's half-afternoon. I see
that narrow room, his face moon-desolate
and slack. As for the fitful shaft of light,

pure as fishhook, it is grief
or something worse.

1957

Passing through trees, I believe my friends
children again, driven
heat-mad, loading the car
with too much chicken, an old Coke cooler
whose glassy sides take light
and bury it in ice. Picnic: a word on the tongue,
a cool mint
20, 30 years ago,
long before I met any of them,
before the terrible prosperity
that made us all in the 8th grade put down
the sacred fountain pen for its sleazy ballpoint brother.
The Chevy's hot, windows rolled down
hard against the hard hot wind.
Next to Susan and Peter, a boy
sits—I don't know him—jammed among them, he
watches a fly
go berserk with rage. Someone's mother
drives. Someone's mother
who's had it: every bickering minute
crowding out a life
that was too small to begin with. Chaos
in that car
moving down a summer day in 1957.
Voices that will quiet in so many years,
call lawyers, whisper love
and then deny it—now, shrill brats joyously roaring
their heads off
at every passing root beer stand. All but the boy
still watching the fly completely, as though
religion were real, a glow in the head, a ticking silence.
What of him? Or of next week when he enters
my life, grown sardonic, still secret. And what use
are poems? I won't know him. I won't.

FLIES

Spring, and the filth returns
in little mutinous packs.
My mother-in-law
insists, and brings us flowers
sullen in their ribboned paper, then
blinking wildly out of jars
we set for them like traps.
My son is three, and looks outside.
More spring, he says, pointing to the yard
no longer snow, but sodden,
beaten down like some awful
something leaked
in earth. I know there is
a god for this. We offer up
our restless rootless flowers.
But these flies
or whatever these tiny creatures are
know more about the inner life,
its worthless remedy of remorse,
its anguish,
jubilant and incomplete.

IN STARLIGHT

On other planets, light does not startle
but lies there certain
of the rocks it skims, as coolness knows everything
over water. So many places with earth god names: Mars,
this Venus over your shoulder, then you
spin me around in starlight, pointing,
if it were visible, that's Jupiter. If
it were visible, I think, as roses
retreat in darkness
to nothing but shape, the trellis
a pale scaffold braced against the house.
House. I stare it
out of shadows—chairs around a table there,
apples half-witted in a bowl. My grandmother,
dead some sixteen years, is humming
nothing I remember, walking through the porch
cautiously, as if it were a rabid stretch of moon.
She stops to pick up something
darker than the air. *And there,* you nod,
that would be Saturn. How close
we are. I can barely
make you out. Your arm is raised
against the heavens. *If only it were
visible,* you say again.

THE DOCTOR FAR FROM HOME

At the auction, several men are dying of cancer.
Not six months, says my friend
as we stand in the back of the place,
holding back our bids. An old man
suddenly rises, his face
alert and spectral as a sliver of moon.
He nods and smiles. My friend waves back happily
as if there were reason.

You could be wrong, I say,
walking through the cold parking lot, past
the pickups and the beat-up Fords.
He shrugs, as though, yes, he could misplace
a scarf, even an expensive one.

At our house, his wife is saying: I can't go to him
for my problem. He can't bear to examine me.
We're drinking beer, waiting
for the roast, for potatoes to soften.
On the porch, my husband hoists
our son, spinning him wildly on the faded linoleum.
Through the window, we watch them.

BLUR IN THE ATTIC

I look across roofs,
summer, a fan spinning
its drugged eye into a gable
there: a bed, a landscape
on the wall—woods, all trees and wonder—
then a ledge where a birdnest
murmurs, moss-covered, still intact.

Nothing stirs, but the fan whirls
hot hot in that room, an anguish
so tight it is undisturbed for years, a thorny flame
within the heart, the way the young have
of putting their bodies
into the sad heat of things and staying there.

A boy and girl sleep on, or pretend
to sleep. Bed narrow as a board. That light
I know, falling of an afternoon.
This house is wood and brick and wood.
I'm old. Someone fills the attic nerve

where days I had once sagged and leapt,
cramped, as I read the required dose.
Wordsworth, Musil, Whitman, Yeats:
witness in that room again.
The girl hollows herself around the boy.
Everything begins by being dreamt.

REASONS

In the first place, the sky lit
always, with cheerful indifference.

You were on your way
to a crucial dignity, earned
by remembering everything.

I remember this much: a wooden boat, turned over
in grassy shade, midsummer.
Nearby, the water stirred and wandered.
I still hold it in my head.
My defense. My rescue.

Your pale body disappeared as you swam
to the other side. Glimpses of you
gleaming. Your steady rhythm

and the thought that if I shouted
you'd hear nothing. Enough
to be breathing, roar of blood
in the secret inner ear.

How I ran my days: to no purpose,
the refrain the refrain of crickets

crickets

so I gave up the evening to them also.

***

In the second place,
the boy came between us
like a happy glue. He copies
our restlessness, says
senseless solemn things.
I take him in my arms, say
tree, say

leaf, say
good night yard. So he
waves, unstoppable as cars that pass,
night that crushes.

We are suddenly the memory
and future of ourselves, slipping through
the screendoor
saying, bed now, time for bed.

                    ***

Third place: a continual slow surprise
at your beauty
which is a kind of country.
I take my citizenship seriously. I handle
my passport with care,
your name as ready on my tongue
as body warmth and taste
is there.

I tell you
the air was wonderful near the lake today,
bringing back days
we knew better, but not
so much.

Table of celery onion tomato lettuce.
I mix the olive oil.
You cover the chicken with a kind of blessing,
soy sauce, garlic.

The boy on the floor
rattles a clothespin against the open drawer.

In the kitchen silence, I hear cars
outside. I hear the world, innocent
of us, pass on.

PERENNIAL GARDEN

In the garden, I followed your eye,
called them lamb's ear and primrose,
stroked the small alert faces
turned up like sparks of a distant moon.
And forgot this was an afternoon in May,
forgot I was a woman and a mother.
How high we were, the houses below specks
of angular darkness. You moved
in and out of shade, suddenly far away soothing
the fierce new flowerheads, their
busy electric yellow. Then the moment
passed, and I was human again. Over and over
I asked you names, hungry
for something, as if we could coin color
and substance and scent
right there, out of black earth.
The owner let us roam—strangers—she, trusting
of a certain wonder. Look, you whispered,
look at these lilies of the valley....
In a perfect hush we stood,
world so conscious and all at once
all as if indifferent to us,
as if we had no names, as if our lives, edged
and thick and dragged for years behind us,
had never happened.

WHITE ROSE

Once this rose knew too much.
Our grandmothers moved easily among its small rooms
and radiant furniture, our grandmothers
as stubborn girls again, hoarding us inside them
in clusters, grape by grape, saying things
like: not me. I'll never be a mother.

Of course, no one believes such truth.
The rose is a liar anyway, its fabulous perfume
proof—though even the mailman, his eyes
tiny hardened cranberries, slows past its ornate
staged longing for a moment
sweetened, like a glass of new milk.

Then the June solstice falls.
The rose knows how long it's been summer: a few weeks,
a whole lifetime. Its scent is the whispered word by now
for confusion, for misery, for love. It leans back
against its stem like a spoiled daughter
anxious to please only the boy who wouldn't dream
of touching her. Slowly the street quiets.

It is barely light. Stars fill the sky
several as thorns.

PURPLE IRIS

To cool off summer, we picked up fans
on my grandfather's porch. Winter, as if we could
invent it with our stories,
my brother's breathless lies: icebergs
grinding holes in our meager boats. He said
it froze us, solid.
Penguins looked on, without sympathy
or amazement. We agreed: frozen so, we'd be
ice. We could see
right through each other.

I know that part's true. For now when we argue,
I can sit here opposite you in the kitchen
and see right through your ice
to the yard, its shimmer of maple, the lingering
lunging crab apple, past that
to the violet bed, its web of heart-shaped leaves
flickering like a pool. Then one dark iris,
probably there by accident, high as radar
on its filament stem. I look
through you and see it,
a rinse of light, a perennial startle
of invention and courtesy, and I forget
we are angry, forget we have done this
damage to ourselves.

BLEEDING HEART

Halfway through the ruined afternoon, the girl
decides to cry all the way through supper.
But why this plant along the hedge
weeps at all, how
its runway of ash and tears
breaks off neatly below the heart, like a pruned twig,
is habit too near
our brain's cool photography. So I passed
the bleeding heart today, one left
on my neighbor's high full bush.
It hung there
like a locket. What I didn't see
till now, till coming home near dark,
is how through this keyhole
a summer parlor shifts and creaks in wind,
the lost piano,
the little wooden stool
turning on its strange, uncertain stem.

MONKSHOOD

They have their vows: emptiness and clarity
and disbelief. In all their immigration,
greed is a country
they never enter. Ancient as chant,
in single lines, they hunch
their small blue heads
above the garden too rash with yellow
anthemis. Monkshood never equates envy

with desire. They envy nothing, not
the sultry peony too rich
for its own stalk, bent down with the lurid
possibility of a Chinese screen luminous
with wings. Enough, they say,
cut back to shroud.
Then it's camera quiet. Shady. Deep now
with other lifetimes, bees
a sudden narcotic. They glaze the garden.

DELPHINIUM

Near the exquisite vulgarity of the chickens,
delphinium casts passion
inward, until it purples
into rich targets. This one is lame, splinted up
with a split rod, quickly
like someone lit a fuse and stepped back.

All day the wind's been low static
and near the house the sound
of men fixing the chain saw. Delphinium
could care. About this, or rain,
or the chickens busy complaining, outraged
about everything, and dropping themselves
fitfully into mounds of dust. They'd bury themselves
if they could, eyeing the woods
through their little ball bearings.

The delphinium never angers.
It learns quietly, by rote: stars
are stars. Better to keep grass down, forestalling
violence. The pine is a brother, sardonic
and plain. Genius deepens, a deep

blue thing, too rapid
to see completely. I am this blue, the delphinium knows
vaguely, I am
poisonous. The delphinium loves
the sound of that: *poisonous*, like the true gift
perpetually offered.

WINE LILY

Bees do not care how delicately
the lily's trance
is inlaid, overrunning the garden
easily, the deepest color
in a bruise. One looks away, for this
is utterly private.
The bees will have their communion.
They come for miles, their wooden hive
stacked up in a low field dropping straight
into woods. Across that road,
the town's violinist
teaches children to sound
like crickets. They'll get better
in a lifetime. The bees have
forty-two days. So sunstruck now, they
can barely figure
the scheme of things: how much honey
by dusk, how much sweet depth
for beauty this obvious. They love their rage
and drop it like a dress
for heaven. This terrible red
lasts for days, the lily basking in air.
How the bees release themselves
and rise across the human surface
exhausted, as if they were skating,
pulled by moonlight, home.

ANGELS

The boy empties the library when he leaves it,
pushing in his chair, not a crumb of eraser behind,
not a splinter of pencil. I bury my head
in the entry for snow, the *Britannica*, volume Sa-St,
thinking: what use is memory
thinking: of course he's an angel
thinking: he will not know it for a great long time.

Old cars. Computers. Then girls.
His heart will stop
a thousand afternoons, the light
half perfect in the television pulse,
all that inertia, plugged in and blaring,
until everything narrows to the sexual instant.

I know he's an angel
like I know certain clouds
new to the neighborhood whose shapes
startle and shame us with their beauty,
moving forward on our lifetimes
with their grand so what.

Then his undershirt, off white,
so badly worn, it cries out
like a devoted younger brother. I hear it
clearly from here, deep into this paragraph, grief-winged
and wet and boring: *slush*,
its whereabouts uncertain, its ambition
amounting, frankly, to nothing—winter
past the brink into a blotchy, cranky child. I keep

reading. He is walking by. For to notice him
is to change him. Angels
know the eyes begin deep within the brain, which
is never human. For centuries, they
have been here, and they call
our thawed life a figure of speech,
onomatopoeia, a fake.

NOON

—*after a painting by Doris Lee, 1935*

She's new at this, that's clear. In studied collapse
against the haymound, she aches to agree, has
almost agreed to everything he glorifies: summer, a guy
taking his shirt off, two bottles drained
and aslant in the basket. She does not blink
though sun is vicious and unconscious, this moment
he discovers body and breast and the
deliberate gesture. She only half smiles. Maybe he's
not a jerk. There's the corny bandanna, of course,
and his urgent slow motion as if this were
the movies—which is what he
promises perhaps, and the rodeo, and the county fair,
and god knows. All morning, they moved
toward this haymound, a buoy
in waters open and indifferent. Indecent now
to stop them with a human stare, after years,

trees behind them, trees gaining in certainty
as certainly lovers lose it. Every interior leaf blackens
to delicious stillness. We'd say not wind, nor whistle, less
than that, say nothing. The birds no doubt
have their own opera overhead
where her whispers do not reach, nor his slow wet sounds.

Nothing is opaque as summer. As if one could say
what percent of birds were bone, and saying it, know
anything at all.

A CHAIR IN RAW HOPE

The chair sits all night
where there is never moonlight.
The room a thick darkness,
it is difficult to walk.

The chair is simply a chair.
It is our whole attitude toward breath
or weather, toward a good porch
that will probably outlive us.
Someone made this chair. Someone painted it
this awful color. Nevertheless, how
sturdy it is, how sure
of its own awkward presence.

I say to the chair—take this poem—hoping
for some certainty, some
insistence on the terrible with the lovely
which is beauty in our lifetime.

I tell the poem: you are no longer human.
I tell it: you are better than that.

THE RUG

I want to disappear into this Persian rug,
the stilled pale geraniums
no longer blaring their news, past
summer, more solitary than that: stems
in slow paralysis, borders
like roads into twilight, hem of an old
black dress. I suspect we bought this rug
for this: to lie down and forget
a life, see it senseless as a cube
in space, planetary idiot, trash
released out of the cockpit window
into zero sound or air. So we invent
purpose for this rug. I train my eye,
good dog, which moves toward sleep
with only the vaguest intelligence: *this is*
my spot. They want me here. These are flowers,
flat and unshakable and real—ridiculous
parades of them, fountains or pirouettes poised
out of the 20s like a feathery hat.
I say nothing to them. They know
my fate, and go lifeless for me. I drape
my body among them
like a thoughtful, stupid wife.

INTERIOR WITH A VIOLIN

—after the painting by Henri Matisse, 1917

Against the war, the shutter opens only
slightly to let the sea leak in,
its boring livid beauty. An underwater light
in the cool black room, the violin
is half asleep, a warm-blooded creature, its case
bright blue. The eye lets a hook soften
and depart far down to find
this moment. No one dreams
of playing anything, though perhaps
the room itself
is dreamt by the luminous violin. This
or that. Perhaps. Keep going. The violin is always
imagining something else, then lying back.
How the ceiling turns, then stills, to hold
passion here, vented and distracted
in the hot afternoon. There are rooms
we never leave. We close our eyes
and refuse it all: a name, a life,
until beyond, the world can brag of nothing,
dragging its furious, shrinking box.

WALLACE STEVENS AND CHARLES IVES TALK SHOP IN FARMINGTON, MAINE

Neither really liked insurance,
tending disasters
like unwanted pets. After all, there is
no heaven. They know that
now. No weather ever like a postcard, no claim
to solitude. Like any other
day of work, not even exhaustion, all's
tedious agreement,
unlike crickets, like tableau.

They sink into gossip as neighbors do, all
interest in the rose, delphinium, the small blue
forget-me-nots that pine away to pin points.
They stare down
peas and lettuce, doomed
to not quite remember
some crucial innuendo about C
in Key West. It's hot. Stevens
considers taking off his coat, but the dead
are more conservative than most. He shakes his head,
shocked as Ives—at what?
Ives' mouth is a perfect blur: everything

to say, how horns collide
with killing nerve, how these sounds
resist—almost—any reasonable reason.
Yet the truth is
the garden is empty, the July afternoon
a rag. I want to lie here, and let
the world repeat itself in them.
They descend
like humidity, distantly,
like shifting trucks.

THE FUNNY-LOOKING BISCUIT

Imagination is a city,
apartments rented, never owned. Even so
no one hesitates, nailing up pictures, the wall
abruptly wounded,
these watercolors, a local anesthetic.

I finally find a window. They give me tea.
My hosts have pressed into my hand
this funny-looking biscuit and the room
quiets like a homeless thing. What to do, they fraught
over the difficult omelette: so many
guests to arrive on the brink of invention,
inspiration opening like a strange hotel.

But already I've entered the senseless afternoon: not
a wheel or a dish in my head. O street,
none of your cars
sadder than I am, or older,
or more inhabited with such little color.
And the guilty way we all have
on the way to Shopko for something, desperate
for something: immensity and boredom, what friends
they are. I am invisible before them and their fates
are crossing over the glaring lot. I am also too dramatic.
But the light, I hear from the kitchen, just
something to see through.

There, I tell my biscuit, I am happier
than I've ever been,
beauty invented surely as bread is invented
on the nonchalant yeast,
as places come to be slowly,
a stray body of water growing conscious, its boats
absently longing toward a future, as train tracks
inspire godspeed and prophecy. O Shopko!

On your blinding, killing mall, I close my eyes: tea,
a rich pendulum. The kitchen: a clock

that chimes. Voices there quarreling toward a generosity
called decision where nothing
is decided, only one gives in, then
the other, brick by brick,
so the splendid city.

THE WINDOW

The man has finally hanged himself and rejoiced,
sitting down on the bed afterward,
saying kindly: little bed, you're still here.
So the philosophers are wrong, he thinks,
everything's here. I am just as I was.
He takes off his glasses to clean them. Outside
a woman is selling fish. Dead
or alive, he shrugs, she'll always
be a fishwife. He shudders at the stench,
those fish flashing up
their sour nobility.
                    In his long johns, he is frailer,
more beautiful than before, both the man
on the bed, and the man
hanging by the window, blue
on such a day. He recalls falling
into a soft looped rope
and something thickens, a kind of web
around his heart
for passing afternoons. Good god, sadness,
as if this were the opera, he alone
on stage noticing
the unspeakable designs.
Everything's here, just as it was.
And the man on the bed rises
to the window, perhaps
to acknowledge something
over the fishwife, over her
rotting luminous cart, but no, not
to reconsider.

OVER THE TWILIGHT STREET

Fall. And the boys are cold, without jackets,
the football their milkweed pod
bursting over the twilight street. They jump
and release themselves, crying
like birds. Hours from the morning fog,
the air is chilled good water
taken from a stream. They can barely
keep themselves inside their bodies, vivid
as light through leaves, though now
the leaves have their own lifetimes
to consider, pressing back
into trance: a red brilliance
which listens for no one, an iridescence
too complete to translate. I bike by them,
the football spinning above me,
a blurred planet. Boys who will be men,
boys who will be taken by surprise
by failure. Again and again the leaves
enact their beauty.

IV

from *Moss Burning,* 1993

THEN

Each of us had an angel. I say that now
without doubt. What does one say
to an angel, I thought, I who
never had a thought, going home
the street suddenly unreal
with both of us walking. Ahead, the bigger boys
hurled stones and shouted. Their angels—
how to imagine their beauty
unless it be anger. Embarrassing, this secret,
belief like a boat, like an odd translation
of what one thought
an ordinary word. By Mr. Glimm's crabapple,
I made them out, three
wary creatures standing at an angle,
idly lifting off the small fruits.
I dare not speak. I dare not.
Easier to imagine old men into infants,
sand back into stone. I walked past
the Ingolias' house, Mickey out there
with his big front teeth, a nervous glaring boy—
a suicide, but that was later—kicking grass
down to dirt, into dirty clouds.
Already, late summer. On the roof, his angel
draped himself over the gable, not really a gable,
the roof rising up only a little.

THE LUXOR BATHS

Before its high red brick,
a street typical of Chicago: rusted cars
and on either side, stores
boarded up, one still selling furniture cheap
and groceries in the back, and the liquor place
too busy, though the men walked past us
slowly and alone, their new bottles
in paper sacks, and singing.
                              I suppose I thought it
a movie set. I was that young.
My friend had brought me, her father
going for decades, cutting deals
on paint in the Russian bath, and even
the hotter Turkish bath, or for the new guys
who couldn't take it, the Finnish bath
with its pure, dry heat.
He was dead three years and I thought of him,
how he must have hated Wednesdays,
Ladies Night. The bored clerk behind the grill
issued us each Ivory soap,
and to wear—a sheet and a towel
for our $1.50
then slid back to her magazine.
                              It was like Riverview, walking in,
it was the fun house, Aladdin's Castle, the narrow stairs,
and that floor, all splinters and dark dust
until a room opened—full light, and in three languages, shouts
then laughter, and rows of lockers that didn't
quite close. This place—a hundred years old,
my friend whispered, more as fact
than devotion. She'd been there, after all; she'd grown up
with someone who called out
every Monday after supper, I'm going—
meaning, the Luxor,
getting in his big car, headed south toward the Loop.
I forgot to say it was snowing. It was
February, so the wet warmth
did something fuzzy to my head.

I mean, I felt faint, not sick,
or maybe it was the thought
of taking off my clothes.
                              We undressed quickly,
and hurried the narrow sheet around us, such sheet
there was. But really, I wanted
to look at them, the women. At 19, we were the youngest,
too new, too empty, and hardly worth
the effort of a question
though I feared they'd talk to us—
worried they'd *be polite*, these women
too busy with each other
and the car wreck, and so-and-so's lousy husband,
and the horse's ass of a brother-in-law
who walked out, just like that, and Irene,
what the hell would she do now?
                              I love my sister, Irene's
sister said, *that s.o.b....* We were walking
toward the Russian bath, that is, they
were walking. My friend nodded,
and we tagged along. In that webby, steamy room,
she and I wore our sheets, the only ones, ten of us
on wooden benches. I wanted more
about Irene. But her sister
kept shaking her head, *that s.o.b.,*
until a woman got up and dragged the barrel of water
and oak leaves to the center—Snap out of it, Mel!—
flicking a branch over her head, the spray
hitting the benches, the sweating walls
—a million tiny whooshes—
for everyone to laugh.
                              I pretended not to stare
but such bodies. I had never imagined
such bodies—huge breasts and thighs, and pubic hair
in lush spreading mounds, full freckled arms;
thinner women with wonderful bellies,
one had a scar.

She just let herself go after the baby came: my mother's
short circuit for anyone
like this. Here, they stood to pour water from the barrel,
holding the small bucket overhead, leaning back
suddenly languid, closing their eyes.

                                   They set me
dreaming this: I was invisible.
But someone turned to me—Do you want to try it?—handing me
the bucket. They were talking, off the s.o.b. now
and onto the priest
who refused to make a sick call
for someone's uncle. Jesus, the nerve of it.
Do they expect the man to crawl to church? It was hot.
I took off my sheet—
standing there, and walked and stood
and dipped my bucket in.

                            The smell of oak, soaked that way,
vaguely sweet and bitter, nothing
like pine. I wanted
to turn my back to them but didn't, lifted
the thing high
over my head to pour. I thought
of the cold outside, and the snow,
and that long blur
of anything
when it first comes down.

RARE OLD VIOLINS

One is my neighbors' and they hang it
high above their fireplace, a stunned
baby, fine hair and inlaid tooth
and anyway, we say *ribs* and *neck* and *belly*
and touch it as if
it could talk back, however senselessly or sadly,
exactly like music.
                        I walk over, afternoons,
and think of my mother's violin made for her
in her father's one brief fall of wealth. Unimaginable,
a violin made especially for a child, and how, years
later, I held it to my body, this
other body, neck and ribs,
and back arched in its nubbed parquet,
spinning out. A spine.
                        My son's at play, inventing
whole lifetimes with their daughter. These
five-year-olds could be thirty-five the way
they talk a subject up and down, diligently, like people
who take the stairs on purpose.
Today, it's "orphans"—how that's exactly
what they are, and this the breathless
moment they discover. Should they sell their last
violin for bread? With mother, father dead,
do they have a choice?
                        Reasonable, I think,
standing in the doorway to fetch him home, and we're
all peering up at the rare old violin. Maybe
it will reveal itself
right there, like a moon startled
to eclipse.
                        But what is it, to choose? Violin
for bread, bread for violin. The children stare
and stare—such longing!—first each other, then back
to the mute violin. In some half-lit room, full
of years, two centuries ago, which ache
was which, and which was music?

THE BERLIN WALL, 1966

In Biology, the old bucket of snow melted
and got off to steam on the radiator—
distilled water for cheap, we said, the nun
at the front of the room muttering
her ancient misfortunes: a Chicago winter, the winding stairs.
That was the spring
most of us sucked our pipettes too hard
and swallowed the hay infusion
and thought we would die. All the while, in sweet litany,
Margaret Woodson swore
he'd show, her German boy "bopping over the wall"
to take her to the sophomore dance.
Still we readied slides
with hair and blood, and stared
those weeks into enlargements of our tiniest selves.
The glory of God, girls! our teacher cheered and harped
over any bright bit—a fingernail or a piece of scab
down to its cellular tweed.
He got over the wall all right. Listen, such letters—
we couldn't help ourselves, Margaret said a week
before the dance, but oh my God, shot down by guards.
She told two of us this
over something fetal, a piglet maybe
or a tiny stillborn cat, cool and bluish
and so peculiar on the table, her *oh* and *oh my God* until—
poor liars—we faked our sorrow as perfectly
she faked grief.
But the ambition of it, history the least of it—those guards
we invented anyway, brutal as fathers,
and the lover, and the distant wire.
It was a table scarred for years
by bored and quiet girls. For a moment,
I believed her. I remember one of us
had a knife, the other
a hand-held light.

FOR EMILY DICKINSON

When I stood for a moment
in that white room, vines busy outside
at the screen, I thought
of the moth in you, the rich wool
it desired. I watched it
circle once, twice, nearing
the narrow bed, the little desk
though nothing was diminutive.

And I knew what a lousy daughter knows,
those years ago I lived
not three blocks from your house—idiot child,
bone stubborn, never reading your poems much, never
keeping proper vigil. Regret has its
own insect life, that tedious hum
trapped in the head. It can't get out.

But your house was too high, set on a knoll,
a wedding cake crusted
with legend. Here, eat some, my teachers said.
Each one of them would marry you. Still, once
walking past, I invented flowers
for your garden: the dumb, sweet heliotrope, the dull hiss
of lupine, delphinium's brooding reach.
Among them, you stood right up
and squinted. You who noticed everything
made nothing of me, one of the stupid
and unborn, not even the color
of a leaf yet.

Matty, here's freedom, you told
your niece one ordinary day, locking the door of that room
behind you, locking both of you in.
My aunt once gave me such a box, a nest
of boxes really, all rushed wooden birds
and fish in a tangle, all intricately carved,
each opening into its secret smaller self.
I lost count quickly. Or maybe
there were seven. I looked up,
too amazed to tell her.

THE KINGDOM

Long afternoons in bed, we loved
to talk about the woman
on the El, remote
as a rabbit and that intense,
who froze at every stop
until the train
leapt up and knocked us back.
But she'd
lunge forward in her seat,
pedal in a fury
we never biked with, even uphill
or after dark, while the thing wheezed
and clanked and roared on
to the next station.
She'd ease as the speed let up,
sucking air like a swimmer, shrinking down
to her curious deadpan.

Our room floated then, nearly
out its window
at anything so strange, your arm relaxed,
cool across my belly.
We'd think of her—that woman
wild again, that
whole train back, rattling off
its *here* and *here*
and *henceforth*: Lincoln Avenue, Armitage,
Oak Street's dazzling deadend beach.
Not ours, of course.
Of course, hers. Or so
she thought, glaring *ingrates* at us once
in some station's high-dive calm,
ennobling herself
for the next great surge.

An unmade bed for days, that bed,
dusk settling like sugar turning a water glass
sweet and murky. We thought of her

a lot, the way we wondered
everything: not love exactly, not that, more
what that woman saw, say
when released, she
looked down at her kingdom—
sure those obvious streets, but such alleys,
glittering and twisting....

WORK

Chicago—and the days of the terrible job,
the terrible ride to work above neighborhood
and neighborhood, every window below
caught in the same torn curtain, or so it seemed
from the El, a thing dizzy with its own
volts and brakes. I pressed my cheek
against the glass and kept looking: even the flashing
backyards turned ancient, each
almost a square, pinned down with a chair
tilted backward or broken. How long is anyone
twenty-three or four—endless moment
dragged through its bored cousins. *Years.*

And my job: papers into files, files
into their buzzing slots, day after day
at the great university. Near Christmas, nothing
much to do, my office mate hummed
as she sewed and folded ornaments, her desk
an acre of sequins and ribbon. I typed
deep into the early twilight—poems—and stared
them through. Poor things. It was like walking
sideways into the massive heart—a heart
as big as a room—at the Museum of Science and Industry,
following the dim light
in the blue-pitched veins, that gun barrel
double rap in my head. Someone's
real heart, the guide said, amplified one hundred times.

Coming home, I'd see the man
severed at the waist, and walk by quickly.
Each day, he'd set up at the El, his odd little chair,
his can of frosted ballpoint pens. I once
bought two. Pretty soon—I don't know.
I quit before long. By then, it was summer.
The half-man in his tee shirt
began to balance bottle
onto bottle into a glittering, threatening lace.
Look out, he say, rolling
back on his ball bearings the size of a fist,
careful of us, loving our danger.

TOTAL ECLIPSE

Don't look at it, my grandmother said.
So I dragged the big box with its pinhole
upright and over me
next to the garden.
                    All shade in there,
the raw scent of cardboard, the feel
of July like fur.
I waited in my dumb animal doze, watched
the point of light on the inside wall
narrow and cut back,
oblong to arc, a sliver of moon, this sun before
darkness took
the whole box with it. Not fast though,
slow as a mile in such heat,
as a girl walking it
with nothing in her head.
                    But night flooded everywhere
the brilliant afternoon had been.
I raised the box to see it, color faded from the garden,
blood gone out of the roses. I could tell
flowers, merely thicker
than the vines.
            So hot—
I lay down in the grass,
bearable now, night
such as it was, cooler, dark,
and the house a dense, looming thing,
not so far. I thought
of my grandmother inside. I thought,
why doesn't she turn on a light.
                    You'll go blind,
she had said. Don't you
look at it. But weeks I'd invented it—flame
spinning clean
out of a coin so hot
you seared fingers back to bone,
just thinking.
            I see the child I was,

stupid, sitting up, lying back again.
A cricket now and then, tentative,
confused. I half-heard him
where weeds began, all prickles
and tiny blooming knots
closing
because they were fooled.
                              Then it was simply dusk.
A day of it. An hour.
And the moon between the sun and the earth
was a hand on my forehead, a human
voice at my ear.

WINTER

In winter, the kitchen is this pre-dawn gift:
the chipped enamel stove
almost a thought itself after years, there
in the corner dreaming
its next life: not a refrigerator, no,
a red sports car.
But we'd be the old aluminum coffee pot,
faithful and indifferent both,
shrugging off the pride of a charred handle.
Half asleep, I take the thing these days
and fill it up, and set it down again,
measure and measure the coffee, heaped now
to a dark fragrant shape
until the kitchen's held up, a blue-tipped match,
this moment raised, before striking. I mean

for hours it's been like this—snowing.

TOWN POOL

Children bobbing there—
of course they should be dizzy
but they're dreaming the boat's sunk
and the shore recedes, and this
brief life's all theirs, this
once, twice
under the blue water
until someone bumps them, and they sputter
and thrash and it comes to them
here they are, only seven, not far
from supper, their
ordinary beds.

Afternoons, the mothers
lie back alone, or gossip idly on benches.
They don't own these children.
They don't own each other.
Some read a book
whose lurid cover is as accurate
as the way the children
pretend not to be children
but the ageless brilliant who survive,
who let love
burn their lives.
The pool invites that sleepy
double ache all summer, the hill,
past the cyclone fence,
so high and green above the water.

One might look down from there,
the pool no mirror
but frenzy, that vacant blue—
how passion works: urgent, then casual,
then urgent. The brave shouts of the children
belie the inner secret children.
And of the mothers who
lie or sit so still, with
their word or two—one stirs, her hand raised
to shade her eyes. Great change
comes like this.

MAPS

—for David

Those days we had no maps.
I would walk home from anywhere and find it.
The house was something high
as though hundreds of leaves, none identical,
buoyed it up, an offering
above the street, backfiring trucks, damaged
neighbors intent on the next
dark wish. We heard them
humid nights, Miss Starr
in the next apartment, falling over chairs, yelling
get out of here all of you. Get out
of here. Clunk, bang,
then silence. She was past 60, and we
shy as that creature part
of the moon eclipsed by earth, paced
our small adjoining porch, wondering who we were
to do things. You hiked over
the railing, inched along the gable, her kitchen
a few steps more. *Miss Starr?* Sprawled backwards, alone,
she just looked at you, senator for the whole
dumb planet. You too, she said
in elegant burn, and turned away.

That was years ago, and what right have I?
Miss Starr could be dead by now, and the house, who knows,
full of earnest, optimistic strangers.
But you, climbing back that night
into our tiny place, those lines in you
—such secrets in the body—I could follow them down
to the world's first sorrow, and drown myself
as simply as a child might, her parents
barely out of earshot. In that half dark, we stood
and listened at the wall, untangling kindness
from the map of kindness, until
normal sounds returned—a bath being drawn, drawers
opening and closing—and the years
began their clockwork.

NEIGHBORHOOD ROOFS

All summer, so many roofs
torn off and put back—one
three story I biked by,
so steep, the men hanging there by ropes.
Here, one sang, *here*, pointing to a place
past lathe, into simple posts
and beams before I, quick,
turned the corner.

It's just that
watching roofers from my kitchen once,
I saw the old man we hired
move so lithely
on our garage—tearing off and putting back,
for days, the blunt unhurried hammer.
I watched his granddaughter
up there too, though
they never spoke. She put on earphones
and across and down the incline
moved to music. She painted her hammer
blue. Sometimes, raised,
it vanished into the sky's
same color. I walked out one time
and shouted up—water? lunch?
But they didn't want anything,
looking down at me like some dim
distant stars, the night
too cloudy.

Roofers are crazy, a carpenter told me.
I think of the rope that held
those men, the light and air
flooding into that attic
after a century of dark.
To be up there, to invite a house
back to its x-ray,
to the few beams it was—
they must dream everything wrong,

in reverse, and be
glad of it, stripping down
past that first wish to be something
to the deeper one, to be
nothing, before giving up
and building back.

ON SORROW

The way certain people
run through rain at rest stops, the quiet ones
or the quick shrieking ones,
is the way I want
to think about sadness: brave flash
and the weedy grass too shiny in such light,
say, the middle of September
which is always at a slant, the kids
already school-dogged, hitting
every puddle, that slow motion rush
from the car.

But it's the stranded ones there,
old guys with caps, a woman
with her hood up—I look at them
and hardly think at all.
They stand whistling for their genius dogs, dogs
who half fly
through the dog walk zone. Two notes
to that whistling, or three.
Each has a rhythm I can't quite get.
They hunch down
into their nylon jackets, shoulders
already dark with rain.
I don't know
what it is—just what you do
if you have a dog, like
it's raining all day, regardless.

Half the time, I sit a few minutes
in my car before
I do anything. One of them is always trying
to light a cigarette
in the rain. Match after soggy match
flung down. This is hope.

MOSS BURNING

All night and day through summer the peat field
glowed, and turned us back to our lives, these bodies
rattling around the old house
burning quietly, microscopically, just
picking up a cup or going out
to check the mail. I drove there.
I mean I wanted to. Twice the morning paper gave itself
to neighbors fed up with smoke, their clothesline clothes
thick with it, their windows
shut all day, terrible in such heat.
The farmer shrugged: just clearing.
But it wouldn't quit. And then
that breathlessness when a few small fires
jumped water—the ditch flooded
deep around the field to contain it—now
slowing searing the bedraggled corn or another's wheat.

But it was night that concerned me,
how the low moss must look under the clear drought-struck
stars, a kind of idle indifferent burning, as if some
weird lower-depth sea life had come
with their little head lanterns, and taken root amid the twisted
vegetation, slicks of flame
in the billowing rows, quick
as synapses sparking nerves.

Perhaps it was our feverish boy, crying out
don't, and turning in his bed
like old machinery, not quite catching, or you
asleep in your exhaustion, open-mouthed, astonished
at the inner planet. But just then I dreamt it,
dreamt the car stalled there at the field.
It was cool for a change. I sat on the hood
and considered Orion still pinned in winter
under the horizon somewhere, the field
crossing and recrossing
its luminous radar, flash points
in the dark before speech.

That hush—not one word, nothing of deliberate lifetimes.
I could have been a kid gone blank with agony
or joy, leaning back against
the borrowed Chevy, breaking curfew
that ordinary summer before Kennedy was shot.
Or back of that, just a child lifted up on the hood,
squinting into the family photo, caught there
black and white, in a moment
I'll never remember. As if looking through such twilight,
you could forget something. As if you
could put on sunglasses of the darkest sort, and turn
into some young man at Los Alamos, say,
in his sunglasses, crosslegged
and cocksure on the hood—a G.I. jeep
or some beat-up Plymouth—bongo drums
between his knees, poised for the poisonous seizure
of light. We see
through that eye. We close it
to sleep.

Snow, said the paper next. That would put the field out.
It's fall. Each morning now
the children lope toward the yellow bus,
my son among them, until they vanish.
The street goes silent then, as if
they were never born.
But it's burning,
acre on acre, no break in that fury—
so close to here—
too much of the invisible, visible.

TREE

Its disguise was ugliness, and ants
in cheap parade, up and across,
and electric wires cut
right through at a heartless angle
to keep Walter Cronkite on at the neighbors'
so proud of their TV.
                    Thick, thick as too much
of too many summers is thick,
three and a half kids to get human arms
around it.
          In the dark, it rose up
like the drawing of a tree a girl might make
to scare her mother.
                    I was there. I was almost asleep
but the moon—or was it a porch light
left on all night?
What I didn't know
is what I still don't know,
                        that one loves
ugliness as one loves beauty,
which is to say, how the dead love
because they've given up on love: *the ants?
okay, really—broken branches? fine, fine....*

THE STAIRWAY

Once in a houseful, against everything
elusive and too loud, I kept
the smallest solitude.
I could cup my hands and see it, that flame,
a brief blue. Which is to say
I was twenty, dragged along—of course, a party—
my roommate had a new
wild boy, remote and sweet, those two,
as another species. Believe this:

we said nothing, crosslegged on the floor.
But my god—one second
just a wall before us, whole and blank,
it flashed open to a stairway,
stairs in the nowhere upward gloom like some great
bad move, some
changeling's breathless launch.

I turned to my friend—do you see that stairway?—
who grinned at her friend: *Gerard,*
she sees the stairway.
Such racket parties make—in every other room, laughter,
bodies slow and quick with each other,
and the god-awful music.

Is it fair to say now I dreamt this
years ago, woke up
still twenty, amazed at the nonchalance
of certain mysteries: my roommate sleeping, the curtains
stunned with light. And in this quiet, half
a lifetime now. That dream
is twenty.

Outside it's early, and into
a final decade. It's summer, too warm
for morning, the air like something
someone already breathed in.

I breathe it in, who knows whose spirit.

***

If I could dream again like that, turn it over
as we used to hold
an ailing bird in one hand, an eyedropper
careful in the other,
would the dead begin to speak?
Its tiny mouth opens exactly
like a hinge, as each same chamber
of the heart unlocks, unlocks.
Even of things we love, what remains?
Of summer, say, one image maybe—a car,
a gravel road
too little for the map, how
one of us stopped arguing, violent at the gears,
backed up to see that deer alone
and slow, right
at us in the field, chewing the soybean's
ordinary leaf.

All pause is ancient though minutes
speed like light. Forget *coming from*
or *going to*, a story
breaks to threads, worn down by details
until the last detail floats
like a stick in water, two sticks.
That deer we save
for when the room gets dark, his curious look, or how young
he was, stupid, an easy shot
in growth that low, or the wide-brimmed leaf
—this stays—oh, each
bigger than his tongue.
The field shrinks then billows up.
One's lithe
and seasick with it.

***

Not that we could go there. Not that we could
leave this body like a thing
hanging on a hook, and enter like an angel.
Far easier to say
what is beautiful to say, that fields release
their silence like a scent, that any pasture
fenced and distant, haunts
like some pure creature out of Euclid.
The horizon's drugged by that. And years,
his book of perfect shapes, it's open
on a desk until
the cool-tipped pointer in our teacher's hand
glints again like something
launched through air, and shatters.
Dearest ones, she says
not sweetly, is it this? or this?

One makes *story* from what broken bits
one has. Of course the nun was old,
past 80, those lines and angles hers completely.
Give them back! We did,
good repentant thieves, tongue-tied
with guessing. Every hallway darkens then dimly
lights itself.
I ached like that—to mess things up
and be sincere. Once after class,
I seized the chalk, pressed
my oddball squares
and squiggles. Can we prove these, Sister?
Maybe universal laws for these?
Those, she said, they're nothing. Get them off the board.
My nothings, off—off!—my next-
to-nothings. But their manic outlines stayed
next morning, faint map
to shame and joy, two tiny kingdoms linked

by the narrow bridge I stood on.
I still vote
from that bridge; a sometime worthy citizen, I guard it
with my ferocious shrug.

But this dream of strangeness
has a slower scarecrow life. Now I hear it
another way: kids this morning flood the porch, they're true
and funny both. I want their wires, their
flashing discontent with stillness.
They fight to be the dead guy in the play
until the winner throws her body on the porchswing.
No way, they cry. You can't laugh.
You're dead. You can't.

       ***

We hug that fact as though the dead
were always in lament. It makes us the only ones
to be so happy. Don't swear to it.

This first: you have an uncle,
disappeared for years, who dies
an old man but you dream him
young that week, bathrobe-young, the thing
slipping off his shoulder.
He's too radiant to care.

Second, I'll take him back—no pretense—
my uncle then, and I tell him outright in the dream
how good he was, a good uncle.
But I haven't seen you in 20 years, he almost sings.
So what, I say. It was the idea
of you—the opera you loved, the novel you wrote
then burned when you came back from war.
Oh, that. He's laughing, so graceful

in the blousy bathrobe, flushed
with sudden circumstance. Will you come
to visit us? I say. I know it's far, this house
in Maine. *Maine?* he says. *Maine?*
—arms sweeping toward the loosest heaven—
My dear, I can do anything—jubilant, triumphant—*I'm dead!*

Whitman, ghost-to-be
when he wrote his glad insistence
on any beauty, that "to die
is different from what any one supposed,
and luckier"—as if such luck
could free a life
from its saddest nowhere, as if one's crystal ball
looked back.

My dream believes him though, an old man new,
and raised, and roaring, still
one of us. Uncle, after years
I'm dizzy with it, getting up again
in that day's cold light, in that house
we've sold and left, not sure
what besides your happiness
is waking. Just *one of us, one of us*—weird
lovely warp passing
through the stubborn body to its darkest pinpoint:
Tod Browning's film—remember?—six
decades old, *Freaks*, that
little jewel
caught sideways in the throat. It's hard
to breathe.

But in college—forgive me—all my housemates
rushed to be disfigured
and demented, the mutilated, the misjudged,
the film's poor lyric folk
outside the building on the quad where
someone kept it showing. Extra credit for Psychology?

Practical Endocrinology? For Entomology? Really, we looked
a child's idea of insects, shadowed
in the bushes against the show's finale
to leap into the spring's sweet dark
and chant the famous chant: *we accept you, google gobble,*
one of us, one of us, bearing down
on those little Gidget moviegoers our screwed-up
homemade masks, our all-embracing arms, so many, like some
awful Shakti.

Who were we in those twilight seconds?—ancient something
hissing in the moonlit inner ear.

And of the stairway dream? Some dreams are our reward
for cowardice or secrets, the way
we fly, or love completely. But none of us rose
to walk those steps.
Dear Uncle, not one of us, one of us
that luminous or brave.

       ***

So every night we walk real stairs, my son
once so carefully
chanting the litany of the netherworld—his *bad dreams?*
to my *no, good dreams.* His *bad dreams? bad?*
to my cheerful hopeless *good* and *good* and *good.*
Safe to sleep then. Safe.
And the room is any room, all gauzy streetlight shape
taking its ruin
calmly, willfully to dawn.

Of course birds again. But we forget
what they are—old dinosaurs
shrunk down
centuries of morning
to whatever bearable size.

WALKING HOME

Good Friday then,
March, the month to remember nothing
though some of us try—
crocus, and the tiny iris, perfect memories they have
coming up the same way, out of god-knows-where,
the bleak lush bottom of things.
                                        It's the high sweet gloom
of church, this air,
late afternoon on the street, all the flowers going inward,
not anything like sleep. Lamps on in the houses,
one after another until the moon
is just the next lit window
hung high overhead.
                                        Good flowers, I say to their darkness, good
walking up the steps.

ASH WEDNESDAY

—*for Leonora Woodman*

Only vines still loop and twist
and fill the arbor. Grapes—the few
missed by squirrel
and bird—went inward months ago,
shrunk ancient to seed
as they float there.
                All afternoon then
shears and a rake, the little cart
piled high three times now, every worthless
branch and stem
loved too much last summer.
                  I'm slow as a year at this.
Gooseberries, lilac,
clematis back to the flowering wood.
I stand on the brink so long
it's nearly prayer: dear thing in the ground,
sleeping thing, thing dreaming itself
black with frost. I can't think
I do it right. I
can't think.
             It's cut above the bud. It's
cut at an angle, always. It's
cut the odd branches
that will touch, and tangle out light
when the deep leaves come.
Such a dutiful daughter: I do
what the book says, almost.
                But I hardly believe
the deep leaves will come. It's warm
for February, for early March—whatever
month this is.
I bring a radio out here. I set it up
like a god in the garden.

GEESE

They open their beaks and something comes out—
a long ribbon.
And nothing to do with fear, what
they see up there.
It's like breathing to them,
to swoop and glide,
a full bellows in those bodies
gives out a great foghorn.
A boat too lost in the water
might mistake it
for rescue, and signal hopelessly
with a flag, that flag
once a shirt.
To them, such a tiny flapping thing below
on the blue expanse
is—
no, not a wing.
Still their fine broad voices circle
and come down.
Oh heart of the world
briefly,
as the heart is pierced.

UP IN AIR

the plane's all insect intelligence,
the drone and spit of it
in the girls' murmuring three rows up:
the class trip
to Salt Lake. In a minute, they'll
rise and take pictures of each other, shooting
goofy or sweet,
whatever self-consciousness brings
in its instant, stilled bouquet.

Miles below, farms
but no one's working them.
A gate hangs on one hinge, geese land
hundreds at once, in trees.
Don't listen to this. Romance—
half lie, half wish. Not a fencepost
is visible. Up here, one imagines it.

I mean, even the baby beside me
is all blank curiosity, rattling
his keys. Dumb luck
for the dentist and his dentist friend,
and their wives across the aisle—
Oh bountiful country
of a billion rotting teeth.
And now, the tired stewardess is here
and here and here. She's
all business, she's blurry.
Whatever's secret
remains secret, furious years
come to nothing
in this low white noise. But surely

everyone's had a childhood.
And that lake back there
where someone drowned,
and the gate
hanging crooked, and the geese,

well, they're sad too,
and ancient and brand-new.
The coffee cart, it barely fits
the narrow aisle
and the dentists shine, so happy
with decision: cream or not, sugar?
no sugar. One invents
and lying back, uninvents. *Dissolve*
Return   Do not assume.

Below us, by now—Utah.
Below Utah, molten ore.
And still the plane—that roar is constant,
meaning fragile, meaning
about to change.

ARGUMENT, WITH MIGRATION

By Radioville, we were impossible, though the cranes,
they were radiant. They couldn't have cared less.
So many thousands the sky
blacked out: worse than inkblot, worse
than the school nurse, all business, pointing, now

what does that suggest to you? *Suggest.*
We'd got to the woods by then, and their voices
collapsed around us, hideous, like plastic
scraping plastic raw, amplified
by every heartsick turning leaf. Yet these were
real birds, big
strange ones, flamingo maybe, grayed out
by ancient circumstance, and awkward
as they landed, folding up like flimsy aluminum
chairs left out all fall
in the overgrown yard. Wind could
snap them in two, like that.

I was careful not to look at you, and held
the binoculars high until the world
narrowed and got bigger, the cranes
deliberate as monsters, lovable as any clumsy thing.
They never stopped talking.
But how private it was, their descent into the bleak
marsh, cornstalks bent back to a spirit self,
so far from summer. I turned

to look at you, binoculars
still in place. I fiddled with the lens: you
blurred, not blurred. You blurred again and again
as the birds dimmed into
twilight, quieting, dozing off,
whatever they do.

THE SURVEYING CLASS

The young men on a yellow day with lines
and scopes surveying off
the minutes and the corner as cars
crowd past, mute as grand events
that went before—armistices, moon missions,
Charlemagne's last idiot move: this is

a class. We're just walking by. One kid
straddling a fence cries out like a maiden in the tale.
He gets a lot of laughs.
Clerkly wit, you say, going on about something
on the gravest of star charts.

In the mob of students, we hear a young woman:
I just don't think about him anymore. That's it.
And her friend nods dimly.
Always this studied nonchalance. Now they're both
not thinking about him, sure.
And he's elsewhere, not thinking about her either.

Around us, even the trees
are dizzy with lies in every color.
This is fall. We get
used to it: pose, revelation, pose.

HOLY CARDS

A miracle, how the printing press
eked out haloes, and the pious freeze
in each picture—eyes locked inward on some
luminous dot in a head gone dark
as the TV dying to its own
bright pinpoint. We found the gold-rimmed cards
left behind in pews those Saturdays
after funerals as the last
old woman struggled into her Buick
and drove off.

You and I were maybe ten, so keen
on those keepsakes, low rent relics
of the one-most-recent-dead. I turned one card
over to the *b. 1902* and the *d. just three days before*
and the *dear husband, father, beloved brother*—no one
we knew—and the little prayer.
It was Polish or Italian, another planet.
Creepy, you said. Come on. Sad tickertape, they were
mostly scattered in the back
and so many kinds: Jesus holding his heart, its
tangle of thorns, straight out
like a drugged surgeon; Mary
dizzy with visions or accidents
or both; or poor ordinary Joseph distracted
by the sawdust in the shop, wielding an honest-to-god
awl as if nothing bad could happen.

By then, you were scouting near the altar,
no good unless
the men had knelt there, the kind who half-sat, leaning back,
a certain bored tilt to their heads,
and clearly still at the office or sunk
in their slow backyards in those cheap webbed chairs.
They never took cards home. You'd genuflect before
slipping down each pew—what good girls we were—then
turn and flash
a fist, thumb high. A find.

Walking home, we'd count our kill, trade
as our brothers traded a Willie Mays for an Ernie Banks.
We'd do the sappy holy look: folding our hands,
hypnotized, standing just right
between leaves
as the light would fall straight
in that single famous shaft. Those silly, sweetened,
wounded cards. But we saved them anyway,
and looked at them and looked
and laid them out
like solitaire in the quiet bedroom, those
blank ecstatic faces
all gazing back at once.

DISTANCE

The boy swimming, barely swimming, holding on
to the styrofoam raft, thinking he's swimming,
swimming through his childhood like that, thinking
he's doing something—swimming—
                              Now a grown man,
someone else in the lake's
calm center, his boat nearly swamped,
tipping over. The man barely holds the whole business
upright, thinking he's almost there, if only,
thinking yes, this is sailing, thinking he's sailing,
sailing through his adulthood like that, thinking he's
doing something—sailing—
                              Meanwhile, stones over years
lose themselves to sand, and storms
take down trees limb by limb. Birds
are this clear: you hear them
before you see them—
                              Standing here, with my binoculars,
the world caught quick, thinking
this is seeing something: a jay in the elm, the man
sailing, the boy hardly visible
in a lifetime of water, thinking I'm really doing
something, the detail
at such distance—

AT THE Y

In the pool with huge fish on the wall,
light there, and that chlorine blue,
the old women grabbed
the sides and walked all winter
up and down the water, one
with a tube up her nose and taped there,
one with a neck brace,
shrunk delicate as a child, and others—
I can't remember how many.
                              I'd watch their thin backs
breathe as they walked away.
I'd squint
from the skylights. Even a sigh
had an echo there, that sweet water
an eye with no
brain behind it to speak of.
                              They'd smile at me,
so exhausted in the locker room.
They'd smile as they
came toward me through the water
where I stood
and fiddled with my goggles, always
fogged up. Above us
the lifeguard was a high eclipse, in earphones,
his eyes rolled sideways, his body
barely holding in
another body that swayed and whirred
and wouldn't come back.
                              But I'd dive down
to a deeper nothing, pale
as pale jelly, the kind with no flavor,
just the smallest scent. I got so
I'd forget the whole business
in the same tired gesture my arms would make,
the long weight I carried
thinning out to the sound of blood
in my head, that pastoral.
                              It wasn't music,

it wasn't anything at all, only
the going and the coming and the going,
the hard breath between.
I could leave it quick. After so long, I'd
pitch backward against the side
and hang there. We wake from the dullest dreams
that startled way, and lie
down again in the dark.
                    I'd lift my blind goggles—
the boy guard folding towels now, quiet,
bored with his misery. But those women
taking it so patiently, up and down the shallow end
where danger was
exact and unending.

DR. WILLIAMS' DESK

is, of course, all clutter pinned
loosely down—the crooknecked lamp, the window,
so light returns by accident
and by design. The chair is one of those worthy
wooden jobs, fluid on its narrow pivot, the bared
bald-eagle wheels. Carpet, some watery flowers
fading out of chorus
on a deadpan note. Good black and white, good
camera in its sudden shroud.
The typewriter is here, the radiator, both
objects of interior order, the steam of things,
the darkened quick. It seems morning
in this room, the windows flooded with it,
the gauzy curtains
just a gesture. Outside New Jersey and New Jersey
and New Jersey. But real place
and time—inside—I let it float
on my own choked half-light all day.
Lamp, paper, window, books: an ordinary room,
no flash, which is to say
anyone might be walking by, look in,
so what about it. So what. O Williams,
who knew what he knew right here.

AT SCHOOL

They write and read to know everything worth knowing
each fall past snow to spring.
The yellow buses stop
and children wander off, this place a dream
their first dream
empties into. But the teachers,
so real and quick, open their trunks
to the parking lot. Woven bags they carry in,
books, bottles, all business this
early, the dim hall, dim
until they step there.

One teacher doubts herself, and the children
love that darkness.
She stands at the window
looking out so much she could be weather
or a kind of light they've seen in pictures,
scary, depending.
The room slips then, like ice
on ice. They fiddle at their desks,
walk around, know she knows at heart who
they are—fish or giant
ancient squids at sea bottom, not kids at all.
Certain moments her darkness floods
the whole room at a thing
one says by accident
or because it sounded close. They watch her
whisper back
the awkward word or phrase, whatever it is,
whatever hung in the air those few seconds
like a kite wounded,
coming down.

At recess, she's in there, quiet.
She's in there, I know
she is, two of them say, two
who should be out on the playground, screaming.
Not one of them moves

though they want to—oh, they want to.
It's neither happiness
nor sadness
how they lean their heads
against her door that way.

THE CRICKETS

moved their waterworld
under the piano. All fall I came down at 5 a.m.
to their sweet mad hundreds, the whole house
drowning. But each dawn ended the mindless
pull of that water, one oar and one oar and one oar—
B flat maybe if I had any sort of ear.
(My brother with perfect pitch would have turned his head,
listened like a screw to wood....)
Oh, it's hard how human they were, their bravado boring,
eternal, not like a clock though, more
ingenious than that.
Or so I heard once—
if you counted how many per minute, every whirl
and wire, halved or quartered it, minus fifteen, you'd know
love like a thick drink or death's
exact reach or which angels wait with their catapult
for the brain to go dark
as sleep is dark, as years are.
But it's always night in there surely, the body
of the cricket a brief, high explosive.
Hardly any light
but that.

WIND STORM, LATE MARCH

Poor bees, the tree down in such winds,
the gleaming criss-cross combs
in the split hollow.
                    Cold that morning,
the bees clustering for warmth,
stingless in the shock of it, a few
aimlessly rising, the tree splintered—
limbs and trunk in pieces
all over the street.
                    Pearl Street,
and the bees in its round yellow light
wanting only the old
darkness of the hollow, the heat
of the bark, rotting wood close enough
to bury the long flights
though, of course,
                        they do not dream.
We pretend they do, pretend they sleep
hanging there, all wings
and the hard black thousands of bodies
but that time, they were just
stunned, meaning
what now? meaning *summer, and what
use is it?*
                    The men were coming, their
trucks and loud indifferent saws,
bits of honey and wax
to flying air. The bees—not even
angry, soothed almost
by such confusion,
                        hovering there,
hovering. What do we know of anything?
The roar of the men, the same
storm all night....

TO ALL THOSE POETS ONE READS
IN CHILDHOOD

From this distance, any crow
could be the only crow against that dopey landscape—
those good girl books, or comics fading
on each blinding back porch, our mothers
still loyal to things that blossomed
mindlessly all summer, the sweet-tooth pansy, the deliberate
stubborn marigold. But Oliver Wendell Holmes, say,
or Edna St. Vincent Millay, or that Sara
what's-her-name Teasdale, until the last
John—himself—Masefield dropped
dead center into our land-locked state, clearly
a seizure, the way brick streets pulled back, right there
into prairie. How wet and blue, he
dazzled up like foam—I must, I must—and that
sea again, only
a word on a page to us, dense
and imagined as a fly's iridescent eye, but bigger.
Then upstairs once in the flat warm spring,
I opened Sandburg's book. "When water
turns ice, does it remember one time
it was water? When ice
turns back into water does it remember
it was ice?" Such a trade, as solemn as it was silly,
but I pictured a man
staring quietly into a glass
where ice of no consequence suddenly weighed more
than the world. It was my mother out back—
the *tink tink* of her spade—and the flowering plum
just releasing its small
bitten wealth, drifting out
past the alley, too high, yard after yard.

THE BOG

When you came north that spring, we all
got out to look for moose, roads
loopy as orbits in a star book,
and ended at the bog. Our car door
cracked its dead weight once, twice, three times
until the four of us slipped out, our kid
just a little kid but serious about quiet.
We followed out as far as water
bluebells and bouncing bets, Jack-in-the-Pulpit in its
striped pajamas sleeve, and sat so still
we could have been stumps, less and less
as minutes passed
anything we remembered being.
Every time we heard a splash
we turned, all of us, *as if, as if*, but it was
simply bird or fish eager
to get at it. The low buzz of something, the slow rings
of what was hidden but breathing in the water
made us slower until we nearly
buzzed ourselves as though the wish to speak
had sound. We heard crashing
in the woods; you looked up, hopeful.
We heard insistent calls of crows, and a voice
so sleek and brutal, a wolf, I thought—but awfully
far away, I whispered to my son, who *shushed* me.
How long to wait? We'd heard there was a whole
moose family there—mother, father,
little mooslings (is that how it's said?)—and out they'd come
at suppertime if we were quiet. We were, I swear,
that quiet. The buzz got louder
with every rising interval of quiet, which itself
seemed solid as a brick
you'd build with. How many bricks of quiet
make a house of quiet big enough to hide in? To disappear—
we wanted that—so the moose would come out happily,
nonchalant as any humming thing, that is, those things
that hum. Clearly not a moose. The things
one thinks of, sitting in a bog, alert
to happenstance, to marvels—O human vanity—as if
alertness were enough.

THE GOING OUT OF BUSINESS GREENHOUSE

The old lady pauses above the register.
I think it's
forgetfulness or grief.
It's stuck, says the other right behind her.
They pitch forward
to see better—diggers
at some neolithic site.

Such a place, out on a dirt road. Chicory
floods the whole way there. This old thing, says one.
And they look at me
and my potting soil. The money feels
stupid in my hand.

They can't get it open. Well, says the other,
and sits down. The light
everywhere is green and broken. She begins
folding up a garden magazine to make
a fan. I think of those orphans out back: coreopsis
and balloon flower and the sullen somber rose.
We've killed off
most of the plants, the first woman tells me,
rather triumphant. The other is
nodding. She fans herself
wildly with the colorful bent page.

I see you're closing, I say lamely,
by way of sympathy, some start
to it. Oh that, says the standing one.
It's just our habit, says the other,
the fan still blurring.
We're good at it, adds the first.
Good at what? Closing? Doing in the stock?
I wait for their laughter
to tell me. But we're done.

Hoes and rakes and trellises....
It's private as dust
in there.

IN APRIL

Near the bike racks, a dog
is losing his mind, thinking—what?—
that life as a dog
isn't one big bone, days are short,
and memory is a complicated scent.

Believe this too: everyone
is cheerful—it's April—printed flowers
all over their corny short-shorts.
Up the street, another stand of trees, and another
and another on that high hairline.
Tree thoughts, straight
out of the head, though a little redundant.
But nothing's really in leaf. Limbs still sway and creak,
twigs in the buff: the mind's
a genie in its bone bare socket.

The dog keeps at it—sniffing.
I see right through to his ribs, through the ribs
to the soft parts, all order and pulse—
of course, the buried heart
where all dark liquid begins.

V

from *A Stick that Breaks and Breaks,* 1997

OMENS

First thought, the roof's edge and a bird there, singing.
Second, slight fissure in the egg.
Then I noticed light: tornado light, my husband said.
Yellowish. Unblinking. Fourth and fifth, how either shoe
would work, left for right, and so on.
Sixth, a boy sitting at the curb, just sitting. I forget
what seventh was. Then the egg
opened so I could see it. Ninth—the beak, no, the tip
of the beak, past shell. Tenth was everything
lost to sacrifice: the grungy cat fallen, rabbits freezing
in the yard that winter; and crushed by cars, frogs
day by day down to their gritty nothing, or nothing's
pure abstraction. Eleven was
the sound of that: three bells, but mostly after.
You could hear it like you breathe at night
but the thing moving was a moth, in cupboards and closets, wings
done in pen and ink, and done again. And done again.
And done again.

                    ***

So I kept seeing oddball things—old catholic in me
falling down a well. Rethink another omen: small wound
I never noticed but the scar is there
a lifetime. I remember working in a bank,
so bored the summer I was twenty I'd imagine customers
shrunk back to whatever child they came from, easy,
in diapers, or some had holsters, shirts
that snapped, racing up and down—such joy—
in circles. They'd loom at my window then, grown up,
all business. I'd count out what they wanted, knowing
one thing true about them, fished from the crevice only
boredom loves and loves. That egg opens
because a thing wants out. A thing with feet and feathers.
Swollen shut, eyes that make
the whole head wobble on a stalk. How *does*

one cell, dividing? Ancient rope
on rope. Blueprints dream the house, or—
marriage, man or woman, leaf or sparrow, seasick coral,
ragged goat, river rat that knows the rain-soaked alleys
inside out, beloved goldfinch, dear destructive
neighbor boy, puffer fish....

       ***

I'll give you omen #17—as far as I can go with it. After years,
a visit back, a childhood friend, her mother's kitchen, washer,
dryer to the left as we sat below a skylight never opened,
dusky, murky day from that. Her mother nodded
toward the virgin's statue beaming bland contentment
from atop the dryer. And halfway through her terrible rendition,
her husband's death, said, *I was so lost*
without him, pointing, *then*
the blessed mother moved her hand. The man
helped me once, when my father threw my brother out, how
he drove me everywhere that night in snow—not a single
question—to find where my brother, barefoot, ran mile
on mile. So close to sobbing, talk's not
right, nothing's right. Compassion's
not a simple angel but in that darkened car, its shine
was quiet, how every low, familiar house and street
swept by. *Look*, she said, *my hand is*
shaking. Fierce guardian of the neighborhood, her eyes
on mine—agnostic—until
I nodded. Meanwhile, placid, frozen, *she* gazed toward us still
from high Mt. Dryer where below our tiny lives wound
and rewound, backward, forward. Molded shape, plastic
someone poured on an assembly line. A billion,
million Marys just like her. *I saw it, my own eyes.*
I saw it. So swore farmers, kings and hermits, clerks
and teachers, artists, merchants, anyone
sick to death or shattered.... I believed something

sitting there, believed such is sorrow's stone
and ache, that we imagine
every end to it. *I feel peace*, she said. *Like he's*
happy there, wherever. Blueprints in the genes, house
that rises secretly.

So often as a kid I'd lie in bed
and watch my hand turning toward the window.
And play *x-ray*, seeing bone, past
bone to throbbing marrow. Days turn like that
to light. Any omen
is x-ray. Its lens let down
a quiet through the gauzy skylight, quiet
from the car that found my brother one night in snow, shine
without clarity to flood that kitchen. So a dryer
was an altar. So what. So I took her hand across the table,
anyone would, all the sleepless
this for that, the welling up where
no words know.

                ***

But the moment right before—I want back
to that: the cat careful but the long-shot branch complaining, slow
splintering one barely hears. Or the rabbit stretched
in briefest flight. Or frogs
on some ordinary mission, simply crossing roads
for water, summer's twilight, whatever frogs wisely, dumbly do.
Omen 20: the bus this morning lowers pitch as it rounds
the hill. Then someone's hammer quickens
in the valley, nail that doesn't
love the wood, not really, but still
the house goes up. Or this—a dream one night
that flashed me frozen
out of dream, exactly as a life goes out, forget
how many years. It was Odysseus who watched eagles pitch

and hover, marveled at the omen, who was told in a waking dream
to walk inland far enough from water to lose
his sorrow, far enough that anyone would mistake his oar
for a farmer's tool, a thing to winnow wheat.
That such wheat is the color
of my child's hair, or the light my husband waits for
in certain storms, means—
nothing much, though lying there, jarred
awake that way,
I told myself things.

MOMENTARY, IN WINTER

It is colder. More people
in the muffin shop, more now in the library
including the oldest man
I have ever seen. How he sits
so happily and turns the page. What is it
he reads? I can't make it out.

But some good someone has built a fire here.
Call it *hearth*, a word part heart,
part breath, a first last
gasp, the final surprise where a mouse
jumps out of a mouse and shocks
the poor cat.

Poor warm cat. Because we stare
into the fire, and then the page.
But this book on my lap is
a liar—book about flowers, it's all
about failure. Momentary fold, foolish
blinding color in the day's
half gloom. Winter is
too many books upon the table—
thick books and skinny books, a book
of destinations: Spain, amazing
untouched villages in Spain....

From the street, I saw two women
in the muffin shop. Steam
rose from their cups and changed
their faces so subtly I thought how
pleasure is nothing and then
unlocks: not like a clock does, not
how wings or ribbons do.

Oh, blame the cold. There was
a window.

LENT

The second week of Lent I walked
under crows fine in their
calamity, the wide dark wings, the heavy
rusted hinge in their throats.
I heard them once,
twice, too many times. They were a cloud
of bad hooks coming down, complaining.
The path lay ahead and went up,
mostly mud, but water
moved quick under ice, the sound
of anyone crying, then door after door
closing against it. So the light
gauzed over early, from 4 o'clock on.
Lent because of that, or because
of the branches, still spiny and bare.
Into the old leaves of summer I read
oak and *black willow* pressed
into the furrows, the half-frozen bootprints.
Lent because I kept walking, or because
I hadn't slept.

Always, one is told things
after a death: *the woods*
will give way to a field, or *grief*
has its own sweetness, or
she will come to you in a dream
if you ask. But it was all thicket
where I walked, one woodpecker
circling and circling the same
dead tree, probing and listening.
He never left the high wood.
Finally is a word like stone, like
water. Or opening like water and closing
like stone. And finally the woods
opened to a field. I saw
a family there
before distance swallowed them.
I saw their bright coats

get smaller, the children
lagging behind, the mother
turning back to them and speaking.

It's Lent, I told myself, as if
this were reason. For a long time
I watched for larks in the half-light
where tall grass
was bent and tousled like the hair
of a child after sleep.
Love is a wheel and a weight. Once
I slept perfectly, not knowing.

HALFWAY

I hear cars. I hear crows. I hear
the house taking the cold and making it
a bone breaking. All winter these stairs,
and we both give way—my leg
which sings out at knee or hip,

and the wood remembering someone cut
and dragged it to a darker place,
split it into brothers and took from it
its sisters. It could have been a coffin.
Or kept for cheap crates, being pine.

Tomatoes would have given
their summer blood to it. But it was led.
It was laid down straight
to stop all falls. Oddest of places,
neither up nor down. I whisper

to the stairs. Gratitude
is never loud. I praise the awful days
of its becoming. I praise the sapling
buried here. Back of that, the seed
which sent up heartbreak. It broke in half

on purpose. And before, before
the tiny cone wept its resin, the pine
took light from shade to climb
and climb. I wasn't there, but back of praise
is sorrow. Halfway, halfway up the stairs.

SEWING

My mother was sewing: pajamas for us, always,
and curtains for the window
to sleep in. At night she pulled them loose
against the wide backyard where the dog
roamed from plum tree to willow, where
the hammock hung in shade.

But all of it was shade at night
except the moon's full face.
Small umbrellas on my flannel, small
pirates on my brother's as if in dreams
it rained too much
and enough ships docked there
for a whole childhood's worth of thieves.

Years, the same room, the same window.
My brother's bed there and my bed there.
And arguments between us like a wheel
turned to make the other go,
as though one engine.

In the dark, I heard her sewing. Each stitch
a splinter put back and back so rapidly.
Not song exactly. Not pain.
It's the little wizard wayward spool I still
think about, high
and quick—the way it almost
flew, but turned to make and make.

CAMOUFLAGE

The butterfly is the eye
of some greater creature, if we
believe the wing,
the brilliant circle which
watches and watches, waits for
its grisly chance. It's
                     all disguise.
Or the way even sparrows
fluff and rear up
to be bigger. Bigger than
any other tiny bird,
bigger than the next day,
or the day after that
with its freezing rain,
departing berry.
                So the mimics come—
the starling, the mocking bird
which over and over can be anything at all:
a crow or a dove, a riff
of Mozart—scary beast—or a car door
slamming.
              Deception *because*. Deception
since the Ice Age for some.
Secrets in the bones which aren't
whispers, in the fine
and serious brain
whose best parts
cannot think.
              Birds that hiss
from the nest like snakes
so the heart fails
even in a hawk.
              And our own
big cars. Dangerous night, eyes
that blind a deer, stop it
senseless. Not an angel
wielding fire....

CHINESE BRUSHWORK

It's their silence that pools. Then afterwards
students blackening the basins with their inks,
washing off all that concentration. It's
a matter of walking by, nothing in my hands
and finding them deliberately
touching the paper the ancient way, these kids
with their caps on backwards, hair
tied with a band. In the women's john, they hardly
speak above the water rushing the black stones,
the sable brushes. Every Tuesday and Thursday,
their teacher peering over each hunched shoulder
as they do leaves, or they do rivers, or they do
the apple beginning to decay. Ink has its
own creature life, one drop a sudden
artery. The heart isn't far. I held my brush like this,
foolish and solemn, bent like this,
slightly panicked, the old man who taught
bent in turn over us, holding his cigarette high,
taking in smoke, letting it out, curious bellows.
His hardly any English, simply pointing—*too thin* or
not dark enough—our lines leading
waywardly up to make a place to see from. I think
of those puzzles a child might do
slow, in a fever, the world bit by bit—someone
fishing, say, below mountains and trees,
the vast silver of the lake unfurling, an expanse
utterly without detail, dawn or just after
and the teacher's hand on my hand—*no, this,
this*—as he shook his head briefly
like a bird, like someone giving up. I liked
making pears best because some shapes
are comic, some resist you and look back.
I remember my inkstone, rinsing
as these young women do, the long line of sinks
and standing there above the wide black circling
toward the underworld and reaching for the paper towel
and thinking nothing but how I'd felt
the hour pass as a rock feels light, I mean

not feeling it at all. Every time now
I want to speak to them about this fine
and worthless thing they do, Tuesdays and Thursdays,
maybe even at home in the kitchen or at a dormitory desk,
rivers that go on and vines that take the paper
as though it were a place for thought and thought
could climb. Deep contrast—as if that dream
were ever true, the fruit offered again and again
to the frozen instant. It isn't death I feel, walking
by their classroom or seeing the young women
at the sinks, seeing them and seeing how the mirror
gives them back. Something else, though I haven't
a name for it—this thing that opens dumbly
into another thing. A moment, or a shape
that endlessly repeats itself, the way,
walking alone, one who never expects to be loved
might say a name to the open air, and each time
it is hopeless, it is lovely, it is secret.

CRUSHED BIRDS

So many crushed birds in the street.
I don't know why it rains so,
taking the small bodies
down to their bones, just a few
but they are silver.

Day by day, more fall—
a sparrow, a young cardinal
not yet
his true color. Sometimes the head
is perfect, the eye
glossy, no failure in its depths.
It's the wings
that are shattered, as if
in flight, gravity gave way, the sky itself
throwing down this thing
passing through it.

There was one I couldn't
recognize: bits of muscle
tied to bone, a few
feathers awry. Even a cat
would complain. In rain, it looked
washed by every human sadness,
not a heart or a thought, more
what aches and aches—those times
I stood there
and could not speak, didn't say....

HAPPINESS

In the old tapestry, how they float
among the flowers, queen and servants both,
all equally. The vast blue
behind lily and rose
is their permanent element, not as sky
or water makes a world, but as
childhood does, wishing the day
would last. An honest-to-god queen
wouldn't like it really, such weightlessness,
her servants aloft like birds,
obedient birds, just
barely. All this is
dream—ours, when we think about the past.
Or it might be the weavers'
simple ignorance of perspective.
As if ignorance were ever simple.
And happiness? I look
into the faces of the queen and all
her servants, at how their bodies
take the scented air of centuries.
They're oblivious—to the flowers set skyward
and adrift, to anything but
looking blankly out. The weavers making such eyes
had to drop one thread and let
the endless backdrop blue
leak in. Perhaps it was a sweet thing, emptying
their heads like that. Now each is so light
all rise and rise.
They don't know where they are, what
land, or who
the enemy.

CAR COVERED WITH SNOW

Before I clear the windows, I sometimes
sit inside. And the stillness is such
that I lose how the day works.
It soaks up
all the steely details: March
ripped out of February, a raw thing.
Sometimes my son has patience.
And we sit a few minutes like this
in the weird half-light. He says: *we're
in a closed fist, Mama*.
Or, *it's like the car's eye is closed*.
We're deep in the brain then,
seeing as the blind see, all
listening. Outside, the cardinal
tinks tinks his alarm call,
his scared call. I hear it: the snow
so terribly white.
And he is brilliant,
conspicuous.

THE VIETNAM BIRTHDAY LOTTERY, 1970

Not winter still, but not
quite spring, and any hope narrowed
to the dorm's TV
in the lounge downstairs, the official
gravel of its voice. And girls
in scattered chairs, not languid or wise-ass for once,
not distracted. Such a little screen: black
and white, and men who moved only
their mouths, in suits that made them
bigger. But the girls kept track,
and each had a birthday
hidden in that quiet like a flame
you'd cup a hand around,
in wind. The wind
was history and its filthy sweep, whatever
rots like that, in one head
or a thousand. On this day, all days
turned a tragic swift ballet. And thinking as I did
no *what if*, no boyfriend, nothing
staked directly in the heart to stay
and stay, I thought merely
a kind of cloud
filled the room, or smoke. You could see it
and smell it: everyone dark-dreaming there alone
though—what?—twenty, thirty of us?
The only light
was dread, one small window of it, with its
vacant men on the other side
poised above the spinning box like those
cheap quiz shows, and you could get
a gleaming washer or a spiffy car, an Oldsmobile
with any luck. Of course
you could. Of course, sobbed my friend
whose boy was suddenly born all wrong,
right on target, though, that moment, illegal
as an angel, already half
stupefied by visions
on a fake i.d. in some bar downtown. The whole

night like that: sobbing
or relief, dead drunk either way.
I fell asleep late to the boys'
roaring home, broken
wayward lines of them, the marked
and the saved, by moonlight or streetlight.
I can't remember which.

THE BOOK OF HAND SHADOWS

An eagle and a squirrel. A bull and a sage.
All take two hands, even the sheep
whose mouth is a lever for nothing, neither
grass nor complaint. The black swan's
mostly one long arm, bent
at the elbow but there's always feathers
to fool with. Front leaf: a boy
with a candle, leaning curious while
an old man makes
a Shakespeare. The small pointed beard
is a giveaway.
                    I always wanted to, especially
because of the candle part. How the eye is finally
a finger bent to make an emptiness. Or that
a thing thrown up there
is worlds bigger than how it starts. So I liked
the ceiling better than the wall, looking up
where stars roamed and moon sometimes
hovered, were the roof lost,
were we lucky
and forgot ourselves.

THE GREAT APE HOUSE

In winter, the smell got worse. It took you like
a soup. The giant glass-eyed ape would stare with such
condescension I could feel again, walking in
out of freezing wind, how small even my largest
bones—poor femur in the thigh, shoulder blades—
though in that look I passed
quickly to ribs, delicate, barely thicker
than my breathing. I could hear
my heart. And closer to the glass, others
come to see him, taunting and screwing up
their human faces to be, they thought,
just like his. I was quiet. I was, so help me, empty
as the great savanna. But apes love trees.
Banana, more bananas. I watched him toss aside the peel
exactly like my British colleague, years later
in Taiwan, would drop her cigarette on our
office floor, saying, no dear, *they'll*
pick it up—when her tiny daughter
went for it. But not exactly that, since his
was an honest kingdom, fallen grace. The ape would
turn away, though not for long. Or he'd languidly climb
and do some nonchalant miracle, rope to rope.
But not for long. He'd come back, stand
and look at us. Rain or snow outside,
everything whirled and narrowed to just
that look. Like taking your eye to a telescope's eye
and losing it there, up the long dark
in hope of stars. The light, always bad, mounds
of hay, old cabbage heads, carrot leaf.
An attendant would call to him from the upper story.
But he'd keep that look for us, looking at some
distant shape inside himself the way one might think
a swollen river marks something in a dream.
Or so I thought, since thinking is mostly
trying not to drown. I know I spent
too long in there. But I was twenty.

THE HAWK

He was halfway through the grackle
when I got home. From the kitchen I saw
blood, the black feathers scattered
on snow. How the bird bent
to each skein of flesh, his muscles
tacking to the strain and tear.
The fierceness of it, the nonchalance.
Silence took the yard, so usually
restless with every call or quarrel,
titmouse, chickadee, drab
and gorgeous finch, and the sparrow haunted
by her small complete surrender
to a fear of anything. I didn't know
how to look at it. How to stand
or take a breath in the hawk's bite
and pull, his pleasure
so efficient, so *of course, of course,*
the throat triumphant,
rising up. Not
the violence, poor grackle. But the
sparrow, high above us, who
knew exactly.

BIRD PASSING

My ears hurt. And I read a book
about the passenger pigeon, thousands in a single tree
and the tiny man in the engraving, outstretched
as a beggar or a saint looking up—
except his rifle and his leer and his 50 lb. net.
The turn of the century: a massive
groan, years on years rolling over like some
sleepy drunk. The dream of the past
is addictive. My grandparents
down there in their 20s, late teens, thrilled
as anyone to write *three*
new digits.... I'm sick

about the passenger pigeon. Once, in the Field Museum
I stopped before a few last
real ones stuffed high and low in their
phony, life-sized tree
behind the glass. Late eighteen hundred
and something. Not long. Maybe
20 years in the countdown, the museum bag slipping
over their heads, not
some kid fooling around
with a blanket. I tried to believe
in their sweetness, lovely anything
doomed. I can't lie. That red eye could
pierce an eye. It was glass, sure. But even
books make that stare famous, the sleaziest

trapper, the sort who'd crush each
head by hand under the net, hundreds—even he
would turn away. Clearly these
were stragglers. No longer monstrous clouds, thick strata
upon strata of them passing overhead—8 or 9
or 14 hours' blackened daylight, horses
trembling in harness, guns raised to quell
whatever astonishment. One shot, it's said 300
would fall, stunned as stone in planted fields
or open meadow. And mostly

left. That's the blistering fact—left there,
bone and feather and failing muscle, thousands
and thousands of others airborne,
for the moment. Eventually hundreds of others.
Then tens. Then the ones in the glass case
I stared at, who
stared back. Cotton batting

in there, and dust. I keep rubbing my ears at night,
like the baby books all say
is a sign of an infant's
infection. *Because, poor things, they
can't tell you.* But past
the faint, witless buzzing I make out
dark's quiet, open window,
rustling of leaves. Another turn
is coming up. I can hear the roar of years
falling, a crushing, hopeless momentum about to slip
into whatever's next. I had
a dream one night. The passenger pigeon's
loves were vast and particular—the great beech
forests of the middle west, countless
stands of white oak and black oak, chestnut, river birch
and elm—nearly all
of it gone. The scent of cumin
called them down, roses, coriander, caraway,
anise. And the salty snails, the perfect barely visible
workaday ant. A litany of things sweet
and small—huckleberry and gooseberry, crowberry, elderberry,
the cranberry, the currant, myrtle with its
tiny bloom. This
I didn't dream but drifted toward, the way
a room dims in twilight and the eyes
give up and turn
backward toward the brain. Most
marked bird, shimmer of feather, red there,
pale blue. I tried

its original names, half-whispering *o-mi-mi*, the way
the Algonquian did. Then *me-me*, for all
the lost Chippewa. *O-me-me-oo*, for the Potawatomi.
Omimiw, for the Cree. *Jah'oow'san'on*,
for the Seneca, who sang the bird in dance,
in gesture. *Ka-ko-ee*, said the Blackfoot.
Ori'te, the Mohawk. *Pachi*, the Choctaw.
Poweatha, the Shawnee
repeated through dry woods or dank. It was
a kind of dove I saw
as my ears throbbed on distantly,
thin, colliding music. Not the dove who mourns
every dawn in the grass, whose black spot
accuses us. But the cousin who
stayed behind, and in the old engravings still
darkens whole slow pages
with its flight.

LIBRARY STEREOPTICON

Two of everything made one, like
it was easy, like bad light
made the afternoon linger. I held it
to my whole head, a mask,
or some weird device
for breathing until I saw
odd things: a bear rising up
beside a sleeping baby; a shiny street
with palm trees, rich and busy
before perspective got it
in the end.

Overhead, the fans turned slowly as swimmers
who didn't care how far
shore was or how deep the murky water. I held
the endless, the stopped,
and loved every sepia thing: books
that no one read, hundreds on their shelves
year after year of summer.
Three blocks away, my grandmother could spend
a whole day making bread, and then
that shoebox full of pictures. Bears
fierce like that
while every fragile thing kept sleeping.

On stormy days, I'd breathe in the petrol plant
miles out on the biggest road, the wind
strange and metal. Bread
and chemicals, books I'd never read, picture
after picture stilled
by 1928. I thought there was
a shining thread
between such things. I thought
I held the needle.

FASTING

Some wounds are made of feathers.
Ask the smallest woodpecker whose neck
cries out a single drop. I was startled
but it was ordinary
tapping, not ice going dark into water
as I first thought. Tiny wounds
in a tangle of branches—the berries
hurt because the snow's too white.
Or wounds blacken the whole sky; one gets
caught, gets soaked in it. I've been peaceful,
walking that way before anything started
though a voice said, the world
is flat, don't sail to the edge. Maybe
I would have believed that, would have
stood at the harbor stricken as the horizon
swallowed one ship
or two ships. Turning, I saw
blood on the wing of a blackbird,
a brief thing in flight, a marking.

TULIP TREE

Some things aren't meant.
Some things aren't plain.
I planted it thinking, just

in case, the giant elms
on either side are riddled old
and ticking, sentinels

thick with shade. It seemed
tiny then. Cars crept by, all
dwarfed it deeper. One brief wind

would rattle it. Some things
aren't meant but we
were careful. The hose lay

cool and coiled and seeped
those nights until the sidewalk
rivered up, or laked.

We thought: in case, in case,
but either side so thick with shade.
Some things aren't meant—its leaf,

half almost square, half some other
shiny figure, lovely to the touch
exactly as a letter turns, page

by page, read outside
on broken steps. I planted in that spot,
laid the hose so close, good snake

humbled by its ancient fall
from grace. It seeped past night.
Cars crept by but kids

walking liked to take a branch
or twig, thinking to play
at knives, or thinking vastly

not anything at all. It was small.
It lorded over nothing
and gave no shade. But each leaf

kept its distant kingdom
of vein and gloss. Insects never
armied it. And the snake hissed its love

all night sometimes. I forgot
and then remembered it.
We passed it daily coming

from the car. Some things
aren't meant. And even dying elms have
their duty, their everlasting shade

coming down like rain to block
the sun. I chose the spot. I watched
it leaf. One reads outside

on broken steps words dark
and light that drift
into the body and disappear.

It slowly turned away
like that. Kids walking by would
reach and break. It lorded

over nothing. Some things aren't
meant, or seem plain enough.
But I forget, then remember it.

LAMENT

At Safeway, on ice, the octopus—
great bulbous purple head
folded over, arms too many
and haphazard, pulled up like someone needed
to sweep the gleaming case *right now.*
Among tidy shrimp
and yawning tuna, it's the sideshow
freak, a thing
stopped and falling through
everything it was, past
strange to terrible to odd, dim star
between sun and moon though
the sky's all wrong, neither
day or night,
this cool fluorescence.

How old is he? I ask the kid
behind the counter, who shrugs, who
half-smiles. I look for the eye buried
in the blue-green folds. So many
eons in there. So many years
like shifting color turned to charm
the eternal underwater where it might
be asleep like that, or simply pretending—
Awful eerie sea life morgue....

But what if I claimed
the body? What if I took it and kept
walking, crossing the dismal
parking lot, its weight against me, dear
tangle of arms in its
paper shroud. What if I stood then
and fumbled with the keys, and gave it
to the darkness
filling the old back seat.
And blessed it twice, the second time
too long and endless
as water. What then—
And who would I be. And where
would I drive.

I PAINT MY BAD PAINTING

Hawaii, 1993-94

The usual accident—
blue wash on red goes purple while
swimmers move beyond me
in the water, down there against the bay's
white rush. They pray
for something threatening.
I know they do. But probably not
the plane, flying sideways just beyond
their looking up.
They miss a wave like that,
looking up.
       Afternoon. It's getting
hotter though the ironwoods above me
release their shade. It's
branch by branch. Still, howbeit slowly,
the sun takes hold
of half the body—one arm, one leg—
and does its bleaching thing, unambiguous,
bloodless.
       Say perhaps: I have
hopes, not many. A few, as in *a few good
nights of sleep*, or *a few*
stray thoughts, rag or paper or all the way
to bone. Now and then a no,
a yes. This painting doesn't have
enough *no* in it, I can hear
the phantom teacher saying
as she gazes past it, out that window
years ago where someone expertly stole
some poor kid's bike: quick angle
of the cutter, steely tic
of *mine all mine*.
       It is
lovely here. One could fill a letter with it,
easy—the blue intricate,
endless, and one can't take

one's eyes from where the islands turn, risen
in the sea, a thing
gradually remembered. As I
watched from another distance once, affection
slow and muffled in me, a sound
the real heart makes. It wasn't a day
like this but fall, and I loved
both women walking and talking and leaning
toward each other on a lower street. One of them
is gone. I can't begin
to know what took
her back. The *no* in every beauty
is half delirious, half
a blinding door. She forgot us for a moment
and walked straight toward it. Sometimes
I stare and stare at things, except

       ***

these mornings in the dark. It's not
grief exactly, lying in the big bed
this corner made of windows, house
high above the valley, the streetlight lights
scattered below like so much
glowing change. Say, 5 a.m. and up this hill,
where the road rounds the Chinese graveyard,
the garbage truck grinds its way
by headlights jacked so dim
you know by sound alone. It stops,
the men cry out—thick, jagged—not
music, more a puncture
of all that nothing that fills the head
in this dream of waking up. They leap
and the truck roars up like a creature
struck. Then quiet in its somber
wave comes back, quiet
the dead own as we own air, taking in

and breathing out the gift,
careless with it

                    ***

though once I had a better story. For weeks,
my great grandmother, Nancy Gill, sick
and frail, moved in and out
of knowing anything. It was my mother's
cousins' turn to watch all night. About 1930,
in their teens, or maybe twenty, Marjorie, then Elinor—
most loved, my favorite—got crazy, the way
something small and silly strikes sometimes,
their holding back, delicious ache, before
rushing into laughter, then holding
back again, again, until they nearly
wept with nonsense.
All the while, their grandmother
lay there—*dying*, Elinor said, nearly eighty when
she told me, *while we*
laughed ourselves sick! They heard
her shift. The girls looked closer.
And Nancy Gill, herself about a hundred,
touched Elinor's face, her own face
a sudden universe
of light: *Sally, oh you've come!*, and slipped away.
Sally was her
childhood friend. *Imagine that*, Elinor said, *I was*
Sally. Our laughter called her back.
And now, some sixty years beyond that moment, this
story is an offering I make, like
oranges we see
on the Chinese graves, my son and I
walking up from school
these afternoons.
                    How many revelations do we get
a lifetime? A declaration

half-whispered, dear funny solemn secret.
My cousin told me on a fluke perhaps,
but leaning forward to touch my face so
searchingly, to be
Nancy Gill for me, she became
herself. Now I wonder at how we all so easily
flower into something *other*, odd
and wrenching slippage
world to world, laughter to that
urgent recognition. Every day we look
for oranges when we round
that wooded corner and come upon
the graves. Recompense, or mourning.
For an instant, they're
too bright for that. They sting
the eye blind

          ***

and private. Like the sound of A the whole youth
orchestra tuning up
takes into wood, a hum
that goes like water, too many years
to count. I watch these
children at violin, at cello, children who
already know a simple darkness
in their hands, a thing that draws the bow
one realm to another, quick notes into
held notes like the swift descent of fever,
its hanging on until one
gives in, and hovers there.
And the young lithe director, herself
half air, half muscle, cuts the dream
with one hand up
                for closure.
But still that world continues

somewhere in the body, in its
moonless night. How many times have I turned death
backwards in just this place? And heard
this sound?   And wanted nothing
but the slow-motion
each memory makes against that *no* and *no* and *no*.
That a certain laughter does it—how? Or the fine
drift of cigarette, or the way
a stranger walks in any hallway to take us
rooms or years away. Same heart, it hangs
suspended as the children go their tangled
note by note that my son will later say
he forgot about and drifted off, waking
abruptly at the end, not knowing
what he played or who

       ***

he was. My box of paints gets smaller. I have one
pocket-sized, and sometimes on the porch
of an afternoon, I arrange the paper and try
to paint exactly what I see—the bananas' shadow
in the broken leaves, the huge high
blooming trees beyond, and further
where the Chinese graves begin. Failing that,
there's the pure instant
when brush hits, and the paper
drinks and drinks until the blue-green
rests there. What I mean is,
so many things unsaid.

—*for Margaret Moan Rowe*

THE DOVE

Not that it's easy to keep certain moments,
not that anything in the underworld
is evident except in shards, in bits
of feathers. How the barred dove came
to Hawaii—the striped one, the zebra one—
I never found out though its markings
are an ancient dappling, a way
to disappear in so much light and so much
shade. My son came home from school
walking. I could see him from the usual
distance, up the hill and past
the graveyard. I waited for his stories
because he liked to tell me things. How he walked,
bent forward under his bookbag, stopping
to examine a stone or a crumpled note—impossible
to tell anything in his day different, that
the fourth grade boys had stalked the dove
to the lavatory slowly so it wouldn't panic.
Of course, it panicked—what wouldn't?—
which made them laugh. A few of them
had sticks, and one a brick. Recess, and my son
just stopped there after kickball. The flash
of the thing, figured out in a second but
too many of them, he said to me, Mama,
I couldn't, too many. The rest of the day,
in class, at lunch, it was upturned wings,
the bloody zig-zag hard against rafters,
down again, the sound of boys
in their glee, keeping it all back, keeping it,
until bursting into the door, into my arms—not
anything he'd done for a while, being older,
the world mostly amusing
or amazing—
And it flew then, a circling
tight in both of us. Soundless. A descent.

FISH

Under the sewage bridge, where everything
turned echo and cool, two men stared
into the filth for fish, though not
an inch of that stream
was blue, not a handful of stone
the right original color, and all
things scattered
like stars—old cans and wire,
and rusted TV tables—no,
never glistened.
But those men had nets and lines,
all the usual stuff: a beat-up
truck braked high
under the long-leafed
whatever tree that was. To be slow
then alert to the frantic ones, big
enough for the shallow part—
they wanted things
with eyes.

So they stalked
and quick, it was smothered
to the silver pail. Hardly a word
between them because anything under a bridge
is endless. A hook,
a net: there are ways
to be haunted worse.
But those fish
that ate whatever clotted thing
lay for weeks in water—

all this time, and still
mornings, or afternoons, light pooling
certain ways. That awful pulse
against the metal bucket. Sometimes
at night. In my sleep even.

AUBADE

Rain. And the birds—one
sings as an acrobat might
fake a fall
downstairs—every seasick turn
graceful unto
the farthest landing. But rain
carries its weight
straight down, as sadness does,
falling through a thought
to flood a room.

Listen to the yard. One song
builds and one unravels. Because I
dare not move, because you're
sleeping now as you never do.
I know that lantern light
in you, and dawn is bird
by bird. Rain
loves it dark and makes
a sea.

HEAD OF AN UNKNOWN SAINT

"Most likely used as a home shrine"
—Academy of Arts, Honolulu

He looks addled, or maybe
the paint has simply worn off the iris
of each eye until everything's
gone inward. Poor thing, life-sized
and left here like a puppet. He's wood.
He's full of curious lines where
someone cut then smoothed, then
cut again, some uncle who was best
quiet at things that could be
praised simply. I'd praise that way.
I'd say: if he looks tired, it's the weight
of goodness, not centuries. If he looks
dear somehow, it's because he loved
everything, regardless of its worth
or its chance for eternity. And the rain
at the window—never mind that it rotted
the left side of him or that insects
made a kingdom of his ear. He heard
their buzzing but it was pleasant, the tree
he'd been, the way he kept
mistaking them for wind nuzzling leaf
into leaf, so long ago, before
all this afterlife....

SMOKING

I don't regret it, not smoking,
though times in my twenties, I couldn't sit
through a movie whole. Halfway,
at the crucial second that weird sucked-up
feeling would come over me, and I'd bolt
to the lobby, find one of those ancient
nubby couches, smoke
going clear for the interior, down every
unlit passage until I was
normal again, fit for all those strangers
on the screen. But still out there, still sunk
to that pleasure, I'd drift into the great
boredom of the popcorn boy and the ticket girl,
that languid ache
of a place when everyone's
elsewhere—if only the next room—
stalled, distracted into themselves. I'd sit
and smoke quietly, and they'd talk
to each other, flirt even. The popcorn boy
always had a trick he'd do, stacking
Dots or Milk Duds until one box, quick,
would vanish. And the ticket girl would
lean into his counter, just so,
amused, disbelieving. *Sure,* she'd say,
and I'm Yoko Ono. Those little dramas of pure smoke,
I miss them—two real voices in those old
wedding cake theaters of the 20s, Chicago, 1973,
before they were razed for a thing
gleaming, steel and glass, when everyone
in the next room kept looking
one way, and by the bad light above me, I was
looking in, or looking down, or looking toward
these two, the dearest nothing
suspended between them.

FIREWORKS AT NEW YEAR

So the flame tells the night briefly
not a secret but the one
private thing it knows. Above houses
darkness is, then isn't....
Fire, down for months
in its paper shroud until a hand
finds a match, the turning year: a compliance,
fierce.
        It's over. Of course
instantly. But the eye keeps on
seeing it there, the high
bright spill. Seeing it there,
and seeing it, what it was like,
that desire.

THE AMERICAN OPERA COMPANY

Forty years running, it boiled down by then
to one backdrop, a garden
faded to an afterlife of flowers
rolled up in Madame's little studio. Below
the lesser end of Chicago's elegant
Michigan Avenue, such muted glitter, and beyond
the ancient lake. My brother, just
a kid, 14, came every Saturday
to be *Aida*'s king or *Boheme*'s Rodolfo.
And the tiny Madame Del Prado,
squeezed in behind her giant grand, played
each riff—again, Michael!—a hundred times.
Then those sandwiches she'd make, something
out of a tin, deviled ham
or corned beef, so salty
they dazed on the thick brown bread.
And of course, this triumph
or that—Venice, Frankfort,
three cities in New Jersey, 1933—such
hopeless radiance on stage, she'd say,
even the men would weep.

Is it the gasoline air that makes
this stay? We all went home in that.
But my brother alone, the El and two buses,
his whole head maybe, a pure B sharp.
Over and over her note at the piano—here Michael,
here—and he'd hit it
and keep it. How strangers burned away.
My brother telling me
years later, the train's odd sad pitch—E flat—
and braking at the grimy stations, a low D
so sudden and eerie. Real, it happened,
but now this much a story: one boy, mid-century,
silent except for singing
in that room of ghosts. The old woman
rapt with—what?—not herself,
not even music. I saw that backdrop once,

how the path lost itself in flowers—nothing to do
with the plot, or with the bursting,
chanting mob downstage,
oblivious, on and on.

SWIMMING LESSON

At his lesson, the child cannot
stop weeping. The huge instructor takes him in his arms
to sure disaster across the ropes
and back, and across
while the other kids get smaller, sitting
on the edge, bored
or terrified, waiting out their chance: it's all
a watery blur to him.
My son and I on the other side
take turns at diving
for the rings—blue and red and yellow
in the water which magnifies
everything but sound. An hour or so, we
squint and glide, giants
to each other, slow motion
in the ancient underwater: *we*
bestride the world, and so on.
But even near the bottom, the ring
almost in my fingers, I hear it—the weeping
endlessly, like a stick that breaks
and breaks, like a starless night in summer
when all there is
is the roaring body's pulse—as the little boy
is carried from half this world
to the other half, his instructor doing
an awkward *it's okay* and *see how nice*
the water is until it's some
blonde girl's turn. Surely it is better
on the solid ledge. But still
he cries and cries. Poor child who knows
what he knows, and we are
fools. Pretty afternoon. Cloudless sky.

OLD BALL FIELD

Birds suddenly forlorn in such a field, school hours,
so the land empties itself
back to simple pasture. A flock of sparrows, and then
another flock descend and rise, descend
and rise haphazard. This one,
that one there.

It's probably the light. Late morning,
cloudy, and the birds too hungry because
it's spring. *It's spring,* says
the silent couple in the dugout, three hours now
of skipping school, and kissing there,
not an eye between them open.

EXHAUSTION

Snow lay like exhaustion
all over the yard. Then why
this thrill waking up to see it
as though some
large mystery had given up
and said *here*.
Snow, the slow boat. The great
tiredness in it
is a haven the way
great loss is a haven.
No one does it deliberately
but one gets brought to this
as though to an altar
at the beginning of winter.
Where I walked all fall aspen leaves,
poplar, maple
stained the sidewalk. Their fate
is to become
something else. One foot and one foot
and one foot. The way
is deeper now and the leaves
are under all of it.
I would like to say
I could hear them, that the leaves
love to sing and have
many songs under the snow.
I would like to say
all kinds of nonsense.

X-RAY VISION

is what my brother longed for, clipping out
his coupon from the screwy comic,
longed for and paid for, one solid
quarter beneath the cellophane tape.
Then he waited day and night
for sight. *Right through clothes*: oh monstrous,
miniature scope in the hand to set the eye
to all things in the world
delicious and forbidden, under something
vastly, boringly
not. *Allow six weeks*, he
kept intoning. Hope, not litany
though certainly it was prayer. (I can
see, cried the trembling
blind man in the movie for our Catholic
fifth grade, our teacher half
weeping as the projector
spit and smoked and nearly burned up....)

At home, it was simply
any mail? Week after week, my brother
sailing through the door. Our poor mother
with her *no* aimed at his back,
exact. I said, could you see
through cats' fur? Through a door
of steel? Something quick like an eyelid,
quicker, like a bird,
like the wing, down to its bones
and glue? *Anything, moron*—he
forever patient, still
patient. O invincible
country, where childhood is,
and faith, a little
masterpiece.

A SMALL THING

Everyone is squinting
at the beach. Sand gives way to ironwoods—
trees like pine but they are not.
And water—the legendary blue is halfway
green, like bronze
forgotten in a drawer. Enormous yachts
so far away seem
small, the way they thinly look the part
of exquisite taste.

Which is to say, here on the local beach,
you bring a lunch or you don't eat.
There's a changing room. An outdoor shower
with two leaky spitting faucets.
That's it. For some, too much
who keep their salt
and go home afternoons, the ocean
still on their skin and tangled
soggy in their hair.

One girl's been here for hours. She's left
a castle now, two moats, the surf
spinning in and out. Its towers
gloat above all turbulence,
like years and years turn slowly
into history. I saw her
father bored, looking out
to the blue expanse before
they turned to find their car in a sea
of cars. The twig?
The twig's a flag.

ABOVE THE CHINESE CEMETERY

Rain, and fireworks every morning this week,
a flaming bucket
on one of the graves they keep
throwing things into. So the family in white t-shirts
bend and bow
behind the young tree rioting
pink blossoms. Hard to know
exactly—except for their blue and white
umbrellas. Except
the fire.
      But slowly, smoke and incense
climb the hill to our house. I pick out of the wind
their prayer chant.
      April, month
of flowers and candy and fruit
for the dead. I've found cake down there
on the stones at nightfall, its icing
an astonishing blue. And Hershey kisses in shiny foil.
And plain bread. And plain oranges.
In rain, the younger ones
are sent to the car
to wait.
      But their parents, still grieving,
work the round of small explosives
to keep the soul heavenward. It snaps and burns and bursts
like a bad gun, like some wayward
stricken drunk shooting straight up. *Dear father,
mother.* What sound in the world
isn't weeping? Even as rain
comes harder or faster, and wind
makes a flickering heart
of the fire.

AFTER SURGERY

I couldn't read. Mostly I'd drift, half awake
because drugs hung limp from the pole,
their little crackling sacks. I'd look up to a nurse
stationed at the door, counting my breathing,
my rising and falling, writing it down. On good days,
I'd catch her and hold
my air back, or speed it up, and *you!* she'd say
and we'd both laugh though it
hurt to laugh. Always, the shunt at my hip,
its slow welling up of blood, little vinyl
handgrenade they'd drain to measure, then
shake their heads and put it back
empty but the leak out of me would
keep up, keep up. I had favorites
among the nurses—one walked me
down the hall each day, a very big deal,
like Columbus sighting land, or Henry Hudson
not abandoned after all at his famous
hopeless waters. Not exactly
happy endings but just to get through
a day of that, and another day, and so on.
Well, there's no embarrassment
like the bathroom with a nurse
standing there, when the body half-works
and drugs rear up in the belly, and whatever
else locks in reverse, or inside out,
or never to be. She was cheerfully
unimpressed by such misery, matter-of-fact because
routine is a kindness, or maybe hope, maybe
its highest manifestation. Manifest: to
make clear, to show itself, from the Latin
manifestus, "hit by the hand." There were times
I stood blank, bloated, down
the long suck of everlasting worthlessness
or where the self just stopped at some vast
nothing—two different things but one gives
into the other, like an uncle and an aunt,
one low-pitched, one high-pitched, one

who kept talking, one who never
spoke to children. I wasn't
myself, as they say. Or I was myself utterly,
for the first time. One dissolves
like a bad pill. One can't bear it
another minute.
                    The night nurse rolled
through such darkness the way certain large women
hover, unexpectedly graceful. She had
a flashlight, checking each hour how
the I.V. was dripping, or if the morphine
was doing the job—not morphine, which made me
sicker, something else—or my shunt, filling up
the handgrenade, whether it was
getting pinker, a good sign. She glided in
on the pale line cast
by the hall, door crooked
a little, but her flashlight—I was
one dim thought, that's all, distant
in that dark as earth
from any other planet. And she was orbiting endlessly,
or she was a comet approaching.

YEAR IN HAWAII

The ocean takes so long
to think about. I was a toad
there, a river thing that got
lost somewhere between one rearing up
and the next, the surf
before it blinded altogether. Distance
stops; one sees the endless line
of something though mostly a boat out there
is simple, with an oar or with a sail.
I never had a vision
about the place. I never thought: this
is the beginning of the world. I watched
birds. I watched the graceless
albatross. And the sea repeated itself
the way blood brings
its bounty to the heart
and the heart knocks back. So much
of beauty is the same. You've seen
the postcards. People buy them thinking
everything worthwhile comes
through a camera lens, and they put them
in a pocket or down the dark throat
of a mailbox someone later opens
with a key. I've watched tourists
some. I've watched how they love it all,
how tired they get loving it, wishing
they were a little farther
down the beach. And the Hawaiians
wanting just to live there, thank you,
going off to work and coming back, normal
things. I was 43 which doesn't mean
much except I wasn't young
and I wasn't old staring into the sea
which changed exactly because it
did not change. There's a way such
beauty refuses to be anything
other than itself, some god
one might have worshipped in another life.

The scent of that worship's
everywhere. The flowers breathe
it back, and the trees are far too
tangled than they need to be, like people
who dream too much, and hour after hour
never stop turning in their beds. I wanted to
sit on a rock and write down something.
I wanted to have a thought
that would throw itself to danger,
a blazing sacrifice. But beauty
doesn't take you places. I liked the rock
I chose. I could see the others better.
They made a little hook out there, and farther down
a coastline. Months of that. And people say,
it was paradise, wasn't it?
And I think of Eden before the original
wrong turn. I remember it now, I do,
though it's not longing that comes over me
but Eve's restlessness again, the way coral lives
near shore, dark and whorled
as a human brain, at risk
and breaking.

NEST

I walked out, and the nest
was already there by the step. Woven basket
of a saint
sent back to life as a bird
who proceeded to make
a mess of things. Wind
right through it, and any eggs
long vanished. But in my hand it was
intricate pleasure, even the thorny reeds
softened in the weave. And the fading
leaf mold, hardly
itself anymore, merely a trick
of light, if light
can be tricked. Deep in a life
is another life. I walk out, the nest
already by the step.

ACKNOWLEDGMENTS

The new poems in this book previously appeared in the following journals:

American Poetry Review: "Bones Not of This Puny World"

The Iowa Review: "Bad Cello," "Leaves in Fall," "The History of *The*"

Field: "Small Yards," "My Uncle Who Hated Zoos Is," "Near Halloween," "I Imagine the Mortician," "The Way the Dying Hear Things," "Little Fugue," "Double Double"

Denver Quarterly: "Science, Book I"

The Southern Review: "Song in Spring," "The Old Mathematician," "Pleasure"

Prairie Schooner: "In the Driveway," "Summer House," "All Those People"

Maize: "Sin," "In Winter"

The Kenyon Review: "Piano Tuning"

The American Scholar: "On the Street"

The Georgia Review: "At Horticulture Park"

The Massachusetts Review: "Elegy"

"At Horticulture Park" appeared in *Pushcart Prize:* 2002.

The author also wishes to thank Wesleyan University Press, which initially brought out the poems selected here in *View from the Gazebo* and *Descendant*, and Oberlin College Press for first publishing the poems in *Moss Burning* and *A Stick that Breaks and Breaks*. Many thanks go as well to Purdue University for the sabbatical leave, the National Endowment for the Arts for the fellowship, and the Ragdale Foundation for the residency that allowed time for the work toward this collection to happen. And of course, to David and Will Dunlap, Brigit Kelly, and Joy Manesiotis for their suggestions as this collection took form: much gratitude and affection.

ABOUT THE AUTHOR

Marianne Boruch is the author of four previous poetry collections, and *Poetry's Old Air*, a book of essays. Among her awards are NEA fellowships and Pushcart Prizes, and her work has appearded in *Best American Poetry*. She teaches in the MFA Program at Purdue University, and has taught in Warren Wilson College's MFA Program and as an exchange professor at the University of Hamburg. She lives with her husband in West Lafayette, Indiana.

COLOPHON

Designed by Steve Farkas
Composed by Professional Book Compositors
using Weiss 11 point text type and
14 point bold display type.
Printed and bound by
Cushing-Malloy using
60# Glatfelter offset acid-free paper